The Survey of Academic Libraries, 2014-15 Edition

WITHDRAWN

Stafford Library
Columbia College
1001 Rogers Street
Columbia, MO 65216

ISBN: 978-1-57440-293-3
Library of Congress Control Number: 2014944847
© 2014 Primary Research Group, Inc.

TABLE OF CONTENTS

TABLE OF CONTENTS 3
LIST OF TABLES 4
THE QUESTIONNAIRE 34
SURVEY PARTICIPANTS 41
CHARACTERISTICS OF THE SAMPLE 42
SUMMARY OF MAIN FINDINGS 47
Chapter 1 – Staff 64
Chapter 2 – Student Workers 72
Chapter 3 – Changes in the Deployment of Labor 80
Chapter 4 – Materials & A/V Spending 84
Chapter 5 – Grants 100
Chapter 6 – Capital Spending 117
Chapter 7 – Technology Education Center 131
Chapter 8 – Books 135
Chapter 9 – Journals 165
Chapter 10 – Special Collections 177
Chapter 11 – Spending Trends 187
Chapter 12 – Computing Devices and Library Information Technology 211

LIST OF TABLES

Table 1	What is the total staff of the library in terms of the number of full-time equivalent positions?	64
Table 1.1.1	What is the total staff of the library in terms of the number of full-time equivalent positions?	64
Table 1.1.2	What is the total staff of the library in terms of the number of full-time equivalent positions? Broken out by type of college.	64
Table 1.1.3	What is the total staff of the library in terms of the number of full-time equivalent positions? Broken out by full-time equivalent enrollment of the college.	64
Table 1.1.4	What is the total staff of the library in terms of the number of full-time equivalent positions? Broken out by public or private status of the college.	65
Table 1.1.5	What is the total staff of the library in terms of the number of full-time equivalent positions? Broken out by annual full-time tuition prior to any deductions.	65
Table 2	What is the total annual cost of salaries, benefits, and other compensation for the library in the 2013-14 academic year?	66
Table 2.1.1	What is the total annual cost of salaries, benefits, and other compensation for the library in the 2013-14 academic year?	66
Table 2.1.2	What is the total annual cost of salaries, benefits, and other compensation for the library in the 2013-14 academic year? Broken out by type of college.	66
Table 2.1.3	What is the total annual cost of salaries, benefits, and other compensation for the library in the 2013-14 academic year? Broken out by full-time equivalent enrollment of the college.	66
Table 2.1.4	What is the total annual cost of salaries, benefits, and other compensation for the library in the 2013-14 academic year? Broken out by public or private status of the college.	67
Table 2.1.5	What is the total annual cost of salaries, benefits, and other compensation for the library in the 2013-14 academic year? Broken out by annual full-time tuition prior to any deductions.	67
Table 3	Over the past year, how have the salaries and benefits for the librarians employed by your institution changed?	68
Table 3.1.1	Over the past year, how have the salaries and benefits for the librarians employed by your institution changed?	68
Table 3.1.2	Over the past year, how have the salaries and benefits for the librarians employed by your institution changed? Broken out by type of college.	68
Table 3.1.3	Over the past year, how have the salaries and benefits for the librarians employed by your institution changed? Broken out by full-time equivalent enrollment of the college.	68

Table 3.1.4	Over the past year, how have the salaries and benefits for the librarians employed by your institution changed? Broken out by public or private status of the college.	69
Table 3.1.5	Over the past year, how have the salaries and benefits for the librarians employed by your institution changed? Broken out by annual full-time tuition prior to any deductions.	69
Table 4	What was the total percentage change, if any, in the number of librarians employed by your institution for the 2013-14 academic year?	70
Table 4.1.1	What was the total percentage change, if any, in the number of librarians employed by your institution for the 2013-14 academic year?	70
Table 4.1.2	What was the total percentage change, if any, in the number of librarians employed by your institution for the 2013-14 academic year? Broken out by type of college.	70
Table 4.1.3	What was the total percentage change, if any, in the number of librarians employed by your institution for the 2013-14 academic year? Broken out by full-time equivalent enrollment of the college.	70
Table 4.1.4	What was the total percentage change, if any, in the number of librarians employed by your institution for the 2013-14 academic year? Broken out by public or private status of the college.	71
Table 4.1.5	What was the total percentage change, if any, in the number of librarians employed by your institution for the 2013-14 academic year? Broken out by annual full-time tuition prior to any deductions.	71
Table 5	How many students work in your library?	72
Table 5.1.1	How many students work in your library?	72
Table 5.1.2	How many students work in your library? Broken out by type of college.	72
Table 5.1.3	How many students work in your library? Broken out by full-time equivalent enrollment of the college.	72
Table 5.1.4	How many students work in your library? Broken out by public or private status of the college.	73
Table 5.1.5	How many students work in your library? Broken out by annual full-time tuition prior to any deductions.	73
Table 6	What is the average number of hours worked per week for the students who work in your library?	74
Table 6.1.1	What is the average number of hours worked per week for the students who work in your library?	74
Table 6.1.2	What is the average number of hours worked per week for the students who work in your library? Broken out by type of college.	74

Table 6.1.3	What is the average number of hours worked per week for the students who work in your library? Broken out by full-time equivalent enrollment of the college.	74
Table 6.1.4	What is the average number of hours worked per week for the students who work in your library? Broken out by public or private status of the college.	75
Table 6.1.5	What is the average number of hours worked per week for the students who work in your library? Broken out by annual full-time tuition prior to any deductions.	75
Table 7	What is the average hourly rate of pay (in USD) for the students who work in the library?	76
Table 7.1.1	What is the average hourly rate of pay (in USD) for the students who work in the library?	76
Table 7.1.2	What is the average hourly rate of pay (in USD) for the students who work in the library? Broken out by type of college.	76
Table 7.1.3	What is the average hourly rate of pay (in USD) for the students who work in the library? Broken out by full-time equivalent enrollment of the college.	76
Table 7.1.4	What is the average hourly rate of pay (in USD) for the students who work in the library? Broken out by public or private status of the college.	77
Table 7.1.5	What is the average hourly rate of pay (in USD) for the students who work in the library? Broken out by annual full-time tuition prior to any deductions.	77
Table 8	As a general rule, how do you expect resource allocation to the library over the next few years to stack up vis-à-vis other academic departments in your institution?	82
Table 8.1.1	As a general rule, how do you expect resource allocation to the library over the next few years to stack up vis-à-vis other academic departments in your institution?	82
Table 8.1.2	As a general rule, how do you expect resource allocation to the library over the next few years to stack up vis-à-vis other academic departments in your institution? Broken out by type of college.	82
Table 8.1.3	As a general rule, how do you expect resource allocation to the library over the next few years to stack up vis-à-vis other academic departments in your institution? Broken out by full-time equivalent enrollment of the college.	83
Table 8.1.4	As a general rule, how do you expect resource allocation to the library over the next few years to stack up vis-à-vis other academic departments in your institution? Broken out by public or private status of the college.	83
Table 8.1.5	As a general rule, how do you expect resource allocation to the library over the next few years to stack up vis-à-vis other	

The Survey of Academic Libraries, 2014-15 Edition

	academic departments in your institution? Broken out by annual full-time tuition prior to any deductions.	83
Table 9	What is the library's total spending on materials/content for the 2013-14 academic year?	84
Table 9.1.1	What is the library's total spending on materials/content for the 2013-14 academic year?	84
Table 9.1.2	What is the library's total spending on materials/content for the 2013-14 academic year? Broken out by type of college.	84
Table 9.1.3	What is the library's total spending on materials/content for the 2013-14 academic year? Broken out by full-time equivalent enrollment of the college.	85
Table 9.1.4	What is the library's total spending on materials/content for the 2013-14 academic year? Broken out by public or private status of the college.	85
Table 9.1.5	What is the library's total spending on materials/content for the 2013-14 academic year? Broken out by annual full-time tuition prior to any deductions.	85
Table 10	By how much did materials spending change (not accounting for inflation) in the 2013-14 academic year?	86
Table 10.1.1	By how much did materials spending change (not accounting for inflation) in the 2013-14 academic year?	86
Table 10.1.2	By how much did materials spending change (not accounting for inflation) in the 2013-14 academic year? Broken out by type of college.	86
Table 10.1.3	By how much did materials spending change (not accounting for inflation) in the 2013-14 academic year? Broken out by full-time equivalent enrollment of the college.	86
Table 10.1.4	By how much did materials spending change (not accounting for inflation) in the 2013-14 academic year? Broken out by public or private status of the college.	87
Table 10.1.5	By how much did materials spending change (not accounting for inflation) in the 2013-14 academic year? Broken out by annual full-time tuition prior to any deductions.	87
Table 11	By how much do you expect materials spending to change in the 2014-15 academic year?	88
Table 11.1.1	By how much do you expect materials spending to change in the 2014-15 academic year?	88
Table 11.1.2	By how much do you expect materials spending to change in the 2014-15 academic year? Broken out by type of college.	88
Table 11.1.3	By how much do you expect materials spending to change in the 2014-15 academic year? Broken out by full-time equivalent enrollment of the college.	88
Table 11.1.4	By how much do you expect materials spending to change in the 2014-15 academic year? Broken out by public or private status of the college.	89

Table 11.1.5	By how much do you expect materials spending to change in the 2014-15 academic year? Broken out by annual full-time tuition prior to any deductions	89
Table 12	How much will the library spend for information accessed online in the 2013-14 academic year?	90
Table 12.1.1	How much will the library spend for information accessed online in the 2013-14 academic year?	90
Table 12.1.2	How much will the library spend for information accessed online in the 2013-14 academic year? Broken out by type of college.	90
Table 12.1.3	How much will the library spend for information accessed online in the 2013-14 academic year? Broken out by full-time equivalent enrollment of the college.	90
Table 12.1.4	How much will the library spend for information accessed online in the 2013-14 academic year? Broken out by public or private status of the college.	91
Table 12.1.5	How much will the library spend for information accessed online in the 2013-14 academic year? Broken out by annual full-time tuition prior to any deductions.	91
Table 13	What was the rate of change in the library's spending on online content/information between the 2012-13 and 2013-14 academic years?	92
Table 13.1.1	What was the rate of change in the library's spending on online content/information between the 2012-13 and 2013-14 academic years?	92
Table 13.1.2	What was the rate of change in the library's spending on online content/information between the 2012-13 and 2013-14 academic years? Broken out by type of college.	92
Table 13.1.3	What was the rate of change in the library's spending on online content/information between the 2012-13 and 2013-14 academic years? Broken out by full-time equivalent enrollment of the college.	92
Table 13.1.4	What was the rate of change in the library's spending on online content/information between the 2012-13 and 2013-14 academic years? Broken out by public or private status of the college.	93
Table 13.1.5	What was the rate of change in the library's spending on online content/information between the 2012-13 and 2013-14 academic years? Broken out by annual full-time tuition prior to any deductions.	93
Table 14	Over the past two years, how has the library's spending on video resources such as films, DVDs, film downloads via the web, and other video-streaming technologies changed?	94
Table 14.1.1	Over the past two years, how has the library's spending on video resources such as films, DVDs, film downloads via the web, and other video-streaming technologies changed?	94

Table 14.1.2 Over the past two years, how has the library's spending on video resources such as films, DVDs, film downloads via the web, and other video-streaming technologies changed? Broken out by type of college..94

Table 14.1.3 Over the past two years, how has the library's spending on video resources such as films, DVDs, film downloads via the web, and other video-streaming technologies changed? Broken out by full-time equivalent enrollment of the college. 94

Table 14.1.4 Over the past two years, how has the library's spending on video resources such as films, DVDs, film downloads via the web, and other video-streaming technologies changed? Broken out by public or private status of the college.................................95

Table 14.1.5 Over the past two years, how has the library's spending on video resources such as films, DVDs, film downloads via the web, and other video-streaming technologies changed? Broken out by annual full-time tuition prior to any deductions. 95

Table 15 What was the library's spending on audio-visual resources in the 2013-14 academic year?..96

Table 15.1.1 What was the library's spending on audio-visual resources in the 2013-14 academic year?..96

Table 15.1.2 What was the library's spending on audio-visual resources in the 2013-14 academic year? Broken out by type of college.............96

Table 15.1.3 What was the library's spending on audio-visual resources in the 2013-14 academic year? Broken out by full-time equivalent enrollment of the college..96

Table 15.1.4 What was the library's spending on audio-visual resources in the 2013-14 academic year? Broken out by public or private status of the college..97

Table 15.1.5 What was the library's spending on audio-visual resources in the 2013-14 academic year? Broken out by annual full-time tuition prior to any deductions...97

Table 16 What do you expect the library's spending on audio-visual resources to be in the 2014-15 academic year?........................98

Table 16.1.1 What do you expect the library's spending on audio-visual resources to be in the 2014-15 academic year?........................98

Table 16.1.2 What do you expect the library's spending on audio-visual resources to be in the 2014-15 academic year? Broken out by type of college. 98

Table 16.1.3 What do you expect the library's spending on audio-visual resources to be in the 2014-15 academic year? Broken out by full-time equivalent enrollment of the college..............................98

Table 16.1.4 What do you expect the library's spending on audio-visual resources to be in the 2014-15 academic year? Broken out by public or private status of the college..99

Table 16.1.5	What do you expect the library's spending on audio-visual resources to be in the 2014-15 academic year? Broken out by annual full-time tuition prior to any deductions.	99
Table 17	Has the library received any grant support in the past year from any federal agencies?	100
Table 17.1.1	Has the library received any grant support in the past year from any federal agencies?	100
Table 17.1.2	Has the library received any grant support in the past year from any federal agencies? Broken out by type of college.	100
Table 17.1.3	Has the library received any grant support in the past year from any federal agencies? Broken out by full-time equivalent enrollment of the college.	100
Table 17.1.4	Has the library received any grant support in the past year from any federal agencies? Broken out by public or private status of the college.	100
Table 17.1.5	Has the library received any grant support in the past year from any federal agencies? Broken out by annual full-time tuition prior to any deductions.	101
Table 18	Has the library received any grant support in the past year from any state or local government agencies?	102
Table 18.1.1	Has the library received any grant support in the past year from any state or local government agencies?	102
Table 18.1.2	Has the library received any grant support in the past year from any state or local government agencies? Broken out by type of college.	102
Table 18.1.3	Has the library received any grant support in the past year from any state or local government agencies? Broken out by full-time equivalent enrollment of the college.	102
Table 18.1.4	Has the library received any grant support in the past year from any state or local government agencies? Broken out by public or private status of the college.	102
Table 18.1.5	Has the library received any grant support in the past year from any state or local government agencies? Broken out by annual full-time tuition prior to any deductions.	103
Table 19	Has the library received any grant support in the past year from any foundations?	104
Table 19.1.1	Has the library received any grant support in the past year from any foundations?	104
Table 19.1.2	Has the library received any grant support in the past year from any foundations? Broken out by type of college.	104
Table 19.1.3	Has the library received any grant support in the past year from any foundations? Broken out by full-time equivalent enrollment of the college.	104
Table 19.1.4	Has the library received any grant support in the past year from any foundations? Broken out by public or private status of the college.	104

Table 19.1.5	Has the library received any grant support in the past year from any foundations? Broken out by annual full-time tuition prior to any deductions.	105
Table 20	Has the library received any grant support in the past year from any private companies?	106
Table 20.1.1	Has the library received any grant support in the past year from any private companies?	106
Table 21	Has the library received any grant support in the past year from any special funds of the university?	107
Table 21.1.1	Has the library received any grant support in the past year from any special funds of the university?	107
Table 21.1.2	Has the library received any grant support in the past year from any special funds of the university? Broken out by type of college.	107
Table 21.1.3	Has the library received any grant support in the past year from any special funds of the university? Broken out by full-time equivalent enrollment of the college.	107
Table 21.1.4	Has the library received any grant support in the past year from any special funds of the university? Broken out by public or private status of the college.	107
Table 21.1.5	Has the library received any grant support in the past year from any special funds of the university? Broken out by annual full-time tuition prior to any deductions.	108
Table 22	Has the library received any grant support in the past year from any alumni?	109
Table 22.1.1	Has the library received any grant support in the past year from any alumni?	109
Table 22.1.2	Has the library received any grant support in the past year from any alumni? Broken out by type of college.	109
Table 22.1.3	Has the library received any grant support in the past year from any alumni? Broken out by full-time equivalent enrollment of the college.	109
Table 22.1.4	Has the library received any grant support in the past year from any alumni? Broken out by public or private status of the college.	109
Table 22.1.5	Has the library received any grant support in the past year from any alumni? Broken out by annual full-time tuition prior to any deductions.	110
Table 23	What was the total value of spending derived from grants in the 2012-13 academic year?	111
Table 23.1.1	What was the total value of spending derived from grants in the 2012-13 academic year?	111
Table 23.1.2	What was the total value of spending derived from grants in the 2012-13 academic year? Broken out by type of college.	111

Table 23.1.3	What was the total value of spending derived from grants in the 2012-13 academic year? Broken out by full-time equivalent enrollment of the college.	111
Table 23.1.4	What was the total value of spending derived from grants in the 2012-13 academic year? Broken out by public or private status of the college.	112
Table 23.1.5	What was the total value of spending derived from grants in the 2012-13 academic year? Broken out by annual full-time tuition prior to any deductions.	112
Table 24	What do you expect will be the total value of spending derived from grants in the 2013-14 academic year?	113
Table 24.1.1	What do you expect will be the total value of spending derived from grants in the 2013-14 academic year?	113
Table 24.1.2	What do you expect will be the total value of spending derived from grants in the 2013-14 academic year? Broken out by type of college.	113
Table 24.1.3	What do you expect will be the total value of spending derived from grants in the 2013-14 academic year? Broken out by full-time equivalent enrollment of the college.	113
Table 24.1.4	What do you expect will be the total value of spending derived from grants in the 2013-14 academic year? Broken out by public or private status of the college.	114
Table 24.1.5	What do you expect will be the total value of spending derived from grants in the 2013-14 academic year? Broken out by annual full-time tuition prior to any deductions.	114
Table 25	How much did the library accrue from special endowments in the past year?	115
Table 25.1.1	How much did the library accrue from special endowments in the past year?	115
Table 25.1.2	How much did the library accrue from special endowments in the past year? Broken out by type of college.	115
Table 25.1.3	How much did the library accrue from special endowments in the past year? Broken out by full-time equivalent enrollment of the college.	115
Table 25.1.4	How much did the library accrue from special endowments in the past year? Broken out by public or private status of the college.	116
Table 25.1.5	How much did the library accrue from special endowments in the past year? Broken out by annual full-time tuition prior to any deductions.	116
Table 26	In the past two years, how has the library's capital budget changed?	117
Table 26.1.1	In the past two years, how has the library's capital budget changed?	117
Table 26.1.2	In the past two years, how has the library's capital budget changed? Broken out by type of college.	117

Table 26.1.3 In the past two years, how has the library's capital budget changed? Broken out by full-time equivalent enrollment of the college. 117

Table 26.1.4 In the past two years, how has the library's capital budget changed? Broken out by public or private status of the college. 118

Table 26.1.5 In the past two years, how has the library's capital budget changed? Broken out by annual full-time tuition prior to any deductions. 118

Table 27 Over the next three years, how do you expect the library's capital budget to change? 119

Table 27.1.1 Over the next three years, how do you expect the library's capital budget to change? 119

Table 27.1.2 Over the next three years, how do you expect the library's capital budget to change? Broken out by type of college. 119

Table 27.1.3 Over the next three years, how do you expect the library's capital budget to change? Broken out by full-time equivalent enrollment of the college. 119

Table 27.1.4 Over the next three years, how do you expect the library's capital budget to change? Broken out by public or private status of the college. 120

Table 27.1.5 Over the next three years, how do you expect the library's capital budget to change? Broken out by annual full-time tuition prior to any deductions. 120

Table 28 How has capital spending on new library buildings changed over the past three years? 121

Table 28.1.1 How has capital spending on new library buildings changed over the past three years? 121

Table 28.1.2 How has capital spending on new library buildings changed over the past three years? Broken out by type of college. 121

Table 28.1.3 How has capital spending on new library buildings changed over the past three years? Broken out by full-time equivalent enrollment of the college. 122

Table 28.1.4 How has capital spending on new library buildings changed over the past three years? Broken out by public or private status of the college. 122

Table 28.1.5 How has capital spending on new library buildings changed over the past three years? Broken out by annual full-time tuition prior to any deductions. 122

Table 29 How has capital spending on extensions or significant renovations of existing library buildings changed over the past three years? 123

Table 29.1.1 How has capital spending on extensions or significant renovations of existing library buildings changed over the past three years? 123

Table 29.1.2	How has capital spending on extensions or significant renovations of existing library buildings changed over the past three years? Broken out by type of college.	123
Table 29.1.3	How has capital spending on extensions or significant renovations of existing library buildings changed over the past three years? Broken out by full-time equivalent enrollment of the college.	123
Table 29.1.4	How has capital spending on extensions or significant renovations of existing library buildings changed over the past three years? Broken out by public or private status of the college.	124
Table 29.1.5	How has capital spending on extensions or significant renovations of existing library buildings changed over the past three years? Broken out by annual full-time tuition prior to any deductions.	124
Table 30	How has capital spending on repairs to library buildings changed over the past three years?	125
Table 30.1.1	How has capital spending on repairs to library buildings changed over the past three years?	125
Table 30.1.2	How has capital spending on repairs to library buildings changed over the past three years? Broken out by type of college.	125
Table 30.1.3	How has capital spending on repairs to library buildings changed over the past three years? Broken out by full-time equivalent enrollment of the college.	125
Table 30.1.4	How has capital spending on repairs to library buildings changed over the past three years? Broken out by public or private status of the college.	126
Table 30.1.5	How has capital spending on repairs to library buildings changed over the past three years? Broken out by annual full-time tuition prior to any deductions.	126
Table 31	How has capital spending on maintenance of IT equipment stock changed over the past three years?	127
Table 31.1.1	How has capital spending on maintenance of IT equipment stock changed over the past three years?	127
Table 31.1.2	How has capital spending on maintenance of IT equipment stock changed over the past three years? Broken out by type of college.	127
Table 31.1.3	How has capital spending on maintenance of IT equipment stock changed over the past three years? Broken out by full-time equivalent enrollment of the college.	127
Table 31.1.4	How has capital spending on maintenance of IT equipment stock changed over the past three years? Broken out by public or private status of the college.	128

Table	Description	Page
Table 31.1.5	How has capital spending on maintenance of IT equipment stock changed over the past three years? Broken out by annual full-time tuition prior to any deductions.	128
Table 32	How has capital spending on new IT equipment changed over the past three years?	129
Table 32.1.1	How has capital spending on new IT equipment changed over the past three years?	129
Table 32.1.2	How has capital spending on new IT equipment changed over the past three years? Broken out by type of college.	129
Table 32.1.3	How has capital spending on new IT equipment changed over the past three years? Broken out by full-time equivalent enrollment of the college.	129
Table 32.1.4	How has capital spending on new IT equipment changed over the past three years? Broken out by public or private status of the college.	130
Table 32.1.5	How has capital spending on new IT equipment changed over the past three years? Broken out by annual full-time tuition prior to any deductions.	130
Table 33	How much has the library spent over the past three years to develop new library instructional centers or to re-equip/upgrade existing ones with new computers, workstations, or other technology?	131
Table 33.1.1	How much has the library spent over the past three years to develop new library instructional centers or to re-equip/upgrade existing ones with new computers, workstations, or other technology?	131
Table 33.1.2	How much has the library spent over the past three years to develop new library instructional centers or to re-equip/upgrade existing ones with new computers, workstations, or other technology? Broken out by type of college.	131
Table 33.1.3	How much has the library spent over the past three years to develop new library instructional centers or to re-equip/upgrade existing ones with new computers, workstations, or other technology? Broken out by full-time equivalent enrollment of the college.	132
Table 33.1.4	How much has the library spent over the past three years to develop new library instructional centers or to re-equip/upgrade existing ones with new computers, workstations, or other technology? Broken out by public or private status of the college.	132
Table 33.1.5	How much has the library spent over the past three years to develop new library instructional centers or to re-equip/upgrade existing ones with new computers, workstations, or other technology? Broken out by annual full-time tuition prior to any deductions.	132

Table 34	How much did the library spend on traditional print books in the 2013-14 academic year?	135
Table 34.1.1	How much did the library spend on traditional print books in the 2013-14 academic year?	135
Table 34.1.2	How much did the library spend on traditional print books in the 2013-14 academic year? Broken out by type of college.	135
Table 34.1.3	How much did the library spend on traditional print books in the 2013-14 academic year? Broken out by full-time equivalent enrollment of the college.	135
Table 34.1.4	How much did the library spend on traditional print books in the 2013-14 academic year? Broken out by public or private status of the college.	136
Table 34.1.5	How much did the library spend on traditional print books in the 2013-14 academic year? Broken out by annual full-time tuition prior to any deductions.	136
Table 35	How much do you expect the library to spend on print books in the 2014-15 academic year?	137
Table 35.1.1	How much do you expect the library to spend on print books in the 2014-15 academic year?	137
Table 35.1.2	How much do you expect the library to spend on print books in the 2014-15 academic year? Broken out by type of college.	137
Table 35.1.3	How much do you expect the library to spend on print books in the 2014-15 academic year? Broken out by full-time equivalent enrollment of the college.	137
Table 35.1.4	How much do you expect the library to spend on print books in the 2014-15 academic year? Broken out by public or private status of the college.	138
Table 35.1.5	How much do you expect the library to spend on print books in the 2014-15 academic year? Broken out by annual full-time tuition prior to any deductions.	138
Table 36	How much did the library spend on subscribing to or purchasing e-books in the 2012-13 academic year?	139
Table 36.1.1	How much did the library spend on subscribing to or purchasing e-books in the 2012-13 academic year?	139
Table 36.1.2	How much did the library spend on subscribing to or purchasing e-books in the 2012-13 academic year? Broken out by type of college.	139
Table 36.1.3	How much did the library spend on subscribing to or purchasing e-books in the 2012-13 academic year? Broken out by full-time equivalent enrollment of the college.	139
Table 36.1.4	How much did the library spend on subscribing to or purchasing e-books in the 2012-13 academic year? Broken out by public or private status of the college.	140
Table 36.1.5	How much did the library spend on subscribing to or purchasing e-books in the 2012-13 academic year? Broken out by annual full-time tuition prior to any deductions.	140

Table 37	How much did the library spend on subscribing to or purchasing e-books in the 2013-14 academic year?	141
Table 37.1.1	How much did the library spend on subscribing to or purchasing e-books in the 2013-14 academic year?	141
Table 37.1.2	How much did the library spend on subscribing to or purchasing e-books in the 2013-14 academic year? Broken out by type of college.	141
Table 37.1.3	How much did the library spend on subscribing to or purchasing e-books in the 2013-14 academic year? Broken out by full-time equivalent enrollment of the college.	141
Table 37.1.4	How much did the library spend on subscribing to or purchasing e-books in the 2013-14 academic year? Broken out by public or private status of the college.	142
Table 37.1.5	How much did the library spend on subscribing to or purchasing e-books in the 2013-14 academic year? Broken out by annual full-time tuition prior to any deductions.	142
Table 38	How much do you expect the library to spend on subscribing to or purchasing e-books in the 2014-15 academic year?	143
Table 38.1.1	How much do you expect the library to spend on subscribing to or purchasing e-books in the 2014-15 academic year?	143
Table 38.1.2	How much do you expect the library to spend on subscribing to or purchasing e-books in the 2014-15 academic year? Broken out by type of college.	143
Table 38.1.3	How much do you expect the library to spend on subscribing to or purchasing e-books in the 2014-15 academic year? Broken out by full-time equivalent enrollment of the college.	143
Table 38.1.4	How much do you expect the library to spend on subscribing to or purchasing e-books in the 2014-15 academic year? Broken out by public or private status of the college.	144
Table 38.1.5	How much do you expect the library to spend on subscribing to or purchasing e-books in the 2014-15 academic year? Broken out by annual full-time tuition prior to any deductions.	144
Table 39	What was the library's total spending on books or other intellectual property with Amazon in the 2012-13 academic year?	145
Table 39.1.1	What was the library's total spending on books or other intellectual property with Amazon in the 2012-13 academic year?	145
Table 39.1.2	What was the library's total spending on books or other intellectual property with Amazon in the 2012-13 academic year? Broken out by type of college.	145
Table 39.1.3	What was the library's total spending on books or other intellectual property with Amazon in the 2012-13 academic year? Broken out by full-time equivalent enrollment of the college.	145

Table 39.1.4   What was the library's total spending on books or other intellectual property with Amazon in the 2012-13 academic year? Broken out by public or private status of the college. 146

Table 39.1.5   What was the library's total spending on books or other intellectual property with Amazon in the 2012-13 academic year? Broken out by annual full-time tuition prior to any deductions. 146

Table 40   What was the library's total spending on books or other intellectual property with Alibris in the 2012-13 academic year? 147

Table 40.1.1   What was the library's total spending on books or other intellectual property with Alibris in the 2012-13 academic year? 147

Table 40.1.2   What was the library's total spending on books or other intellectual property with Alibris in the 2012-13 academic year? Broken out by type of college. 147

Table 40.1.3   What was the library's total spending on books or other intellectual property with Alibris in the 2012-13 academic year? Broken out by full-time equivalent enrollment of the college. 147

Table 40.1.4   What was the library's total spending on books or other intellectual property with Alibris in the 2012-13 academic year? Broken out by public or private status of the college. 148

Table 40.1.5   What was the library's total spending on books or other intellectual property with Alibris in the 2012-13 academic year? Broken out by annual full-time tuition prior to any deductions. 148

Table 41   What was the library's total spending on books or other intellectual property with Barnes & Noble in the 2012-13 academic year? 149

Table 41.1.1   What was the library's total spending on books or other intellectual property with Barnes & Noble in the 2012-13 academic year? 149

Table 41.1.2   What was the library's total spending on books or other intellectual property with Barnes & Noble in the 2012-13 academic year? Broken out by type of college. 149

Table 41.1.3   What was the library's total spending on books or other intellectual property with Barnes & Noble in the 2012-13 academic year? Broken out by full-time equivalent enrollment of the college. 149

Table 41.1.4   What was the library's total spending on books or other intellectual property with Barnes & Noble in the 2012-13 academic year? Broken out by public or private status of the college. 150

Table 41.1.5   What was the library's total spending on books or other intellectual property with Barnes & Noble in the 2012-13

	academic year? Broken out by annual full-time tuition prior to any deductions............ 150
Table 42	What was the library's total spending on books or other intellectual property with Powell's Books in the 2012-13 academic year?............ 151
Table 42.1.1	What was the library's total spending on books or other intellectual property with Powell's Books in the 2012-13 academic year?............ 151
Table 42.1.2	What was the library's total spending on books or other intellectual property with Powell's Books in the 2012-13 academic year? Broken out by type of college............ 151
Table 42.1.3	What was the library's total spending on books or other intellectual property with Powell's Books in the 2012-13 academic year? Broken out by full-time equivalent enrollment of the college............ 151
Table 42.1.4	What was the library's total spending on books or other intellectual property with Powell's Books in the 2012-13 academic year? Broken out by public or private status of the college............ 152
Table 42.1.5	What was the library's total spending on books or other intellectual property with Powell's Books in the 2012-13 academic year? Broken out by annual full-time tuition prior to any deductions............ 152
Table 43	What was the library's total spending on books or other intellectual property with Books-A-Million in the 2012-13 academic year?............ 153
Table 43.1.1	What was the library's total spending on books or other intellectual property with Books-A-Million in the 2012-13 academic year?............ 153
Table 44	What was the library's total spending on books or other intellectual property with all other online booksellers in the 2012-13 academic year?............ 154
Table 44.1.1	What was the library's total spending on books or other intellectual property with all other online booksellers in the 2012-13 academic year?............ 154
Table 44.1.2	What was the library's total spending on books or other intellectual property with all other online booksellers in the 2012-13 academic year? Broken out by type of college............ 154
Table 44.1.3	What was the library's total spending on books or other intellectual property with all other online booksellers in the 2012-13 academic year? Broken out by full-time equivalent enrollment of the college............ 154
Table 44.1.4	What was the library's total spending on books or other intellectual property with all other online booksellers in the 2012-13 academic year? Broken out by public or private status of the college............ 155

Table	Description	Page
Table 44.1.5	What was the library's total spending on books or other intellectual property with all other online booksellers in the 2012-13 academic year? Broken out by annual full-time tuition prior to any deductions.	155
Table 45	What was the library's total spending (including all online booksellers) on books or other intellectual property in the 2012-13 academic year?	156
Table 45.1.1	What was the library's total spending (including all online booksellers) on books or other intellectual property in the 2012-13 academic year?	156
Table 45.1.2	What was the library's total spending (including all online booksellers) on books or other intellectual property in the 2012-13 academic year? Broken out by type of college.	156
Table 45.1.3	What was the library's total spending (including all online booksellers) on books or other intellectual property in the 2012-13 academic year? Broken out by full-time equivalent enrollment of the college.	156
Table 45.1.4	What was the library's total spending (including all online booksellers) on books or other intellectual property in the 2012-13 academic year? Broken out by public or private status of the college.	157
Table 45.1.5	What was the library's total spending (including all online booksellers) on books or other intellectual property in the 2012-13 academic year? Broken out by annual full-time tuition prior to any deductions.	157
Table 46	Has the library purchased e-book readers, iPads, or any other devices for patrons to read e-books?	158
Table 46.1.1	Has the library purchased e-book readers, iPads, or any other devices for patrons to read e-books?	158
Table 46.1.2	Has the library purchased e-book readers, iPads, or any other devices for patrons to read e-books? Broken out by type of college.	158
Table 46.1.3	Has the library purchased e-book readers, iPads, or any other devices for patrons to read e-books? Broken out by full-time equivalent enrollment of the college.	158
Table 46.1.4	Has the library purchased e-book readers, iPads, or any other devices for patrons to read e-books? Broken out by public or private status of the college.	158
Table 46.1.5	Has the library purchased e-book readers, iPads, or any other devices for patrons to read e-books? Broken out by annual full-time tuition prior to any deductions.	159
Table 47	Over the past two years, how much has the library spent on e-book readers and devices?	160
Table 47.1.1	Over the past two years, how much has the library spent on e-book readers and devices?	160

Table 47.1.2	Over the past two years, how much has the library spent on e-book readers and devices? Broken out by type of college.	160
Table 47.1.3	Over the past two years, how much has the library spent on e-book readers and devices? Broken out by full-time equivalent enrollment of the college.	160
Table 47.1.4	Over the past two years, how much has the library spent on e-book readers and devices? Broken out by public or private status of the college.	161
Table 47.1.5	Over the past two years, how much has the library spent on e-book readers and devices? Broken out by annual full-time tuition prior to any deductions.	161
Table 48	Over the past two years, how much has the library spent on books and other content for e-book readers and devices?	162
Table 48.1.1	Over the past two years, how much has the library spent on books and other content for e-book readers and devices?	162
Table 48.1.2	Over the past two years, how much has the library spent on books and other content for e-book readers and devices? Broken out by type of college.	162
Table 48.1.3	Over the past two years, how much has the library spent on books and other content for e-book readers and devices? Broken out by full-time equivalent enrollment of the college.	162
Table 48.1.4	Over the past two years, how much has the library spent on books and other content for e-book readers and devices? Broken out by public or private status of the college.	163
Table 48.1.5	Over the past two years, how much has the library spent on books and other content for e-book readers and devices? Broken out by annual full-time tuition prior to any deductions.	163
Table 49	Over the past two years, how much has the library spent on software to e-book enable computers or mobile devices?	164
Table 49.1.1	Over the past two years, how much has the library spent on software to e-book enable computers or mobile devices?	164
Table 50	How much did the library spend on print and electronic subscriptions to scholarly and professional journals in the 2012-13 academic year?	165
Table 50.1.1	How much did the library spend on print and electronic subscriptions to scholarly and professional journals in the 2012-13 academic year?	165
Table 50.1.2	How much did the library spend on print and electronic subscriptions to scholarly and professional journals in the 2012-13 academic year? Broken out by type of college.	165
Table 50.1.3	How much did the library spend on print and electronic subscriptions to scholarly and professional journals in the 2012-13 academic year? Broken out by full-time equivalent enrollment of the college.	166
Table 50.1.4	How much did the library spend on print and electronic subscriptions to scholarly and professional journals in the	

	2012-13 academic year? Broken out by public or private status of the college.	166
Table 50.1.5	How much did the library spend on print and electronic subscriptions to scholarly and professional journals in the 2012-13 academic year? Broken out by annual full-time tuition prior to any deductions.	166
Table 51	How much did the library spend on print and electronic subscriptions to scholarly and professional journals in the 2013-14 academic year?	167
Table 51.1.1	How much did the library spend on print and electronic subscriptions to scholarly and professional journals in the 2013-14 academic year?	167
Table 51.1.2	How much did the library spend on print and electronic subscriptions to scholarly and professional journals in the 2013-14 academic year? Broken out by type of college.	167
Table 51.1.3	How much did the library spend on print and electronic subscriptions to scholarly and professional journals in the 2013-14 academic year? Broken out by full-time equivalent enrollment of the college.	167
Table 51.1.4	How much did the library spend on print and electronic subscriptions to scholarly and professional journals in the 2013-14 academic year? Broken out by public or private status of the college.	168
Table 51.1.5	How much did the library spend on print and electronic subscriptions to scholarly and professional journals in the 2013-14 academic year? Broken out by annual full-time tuition prior to any deductions.	168
Table 52	How much does the library expect to spend on print and electronic subscriptions to scholarly and professional journals in the 2014-15 academic year?	169
Table 52.1.1	How much does the library expect to spend on print and electronic subscriptions to scholarly and professional journals in the 2014-15 academic year?	169
Table 52.1.2	How much does the library expect to spend on print and electronic subscriptions to scholarly and professional journals in the 2014-15 academic year? Broken out by type of college.	169
Table 52.1.3	How much does the library expect to spend on print and electronic subscriptions to scholarly and professional journals in the 2014-15 academic year? Broken out by full-time equivalent enrollment of the college.	169
Table 52.1.4	How much does the library expect to spend on print and electronic subscriptions to scholarly and professional journals in the 2014-15 academic year? Broken out by public or private status of the college.	170
Table 52.1.5	How much does the library expect to spend on print and electronic subscriptions to scholarly and professional journals	

	in the 2014-15 academic year? Broken out by annual full-time tuition prior to any deductions.	170
Table 53	Approximately what percentage of the library's total spending on scientific and professional journals was dedicated to print subscriptions only?	171
Table 53.1.1	Approximately what percentage of the library's total spending on scientific and professional journals was dedicated to print subscriptions only?	171
Table 53.1.2	Approximately what percentage of the library's total spending on scientific and professional journals was dedicated to print subscriptions only? Broken out by type of college.	171
Table 53.1.3	Approximately what percentage of the library's total spending on scientific and professional journals was dedicated to print subscriptions only? Broken out by full-time equivalent enrollment of the college.	171
Table 53.1.4	Approximately what percentage of the library's total spending on scientific and professional journals was dedicated to print subscriptions only? Broken out by public or private status of the college.	172
Table 53.1.5	Approximately what percentage of the library's total spending on scientific and professional journals was dedicated to print subscriptions only? Broken out by annual full-time tuition prior to any deductions.	172
Table 54	Approximately what percentage of the library's total spending on scientific and professional journals was dedicated to subscriptions with electronic access only?	173
Table 54.1.1	Approximately what percentage of the library's total spending on scientific and professional journals was dedicated to subscriptions with electronic access only?	173
Table 54.1.2	Approximately what percentage of the library's total spending on scientific and professional journals was dedicated to subscriptions with electronic access only? Broken out by type of college.	173
Table 54.1.3	Approximately what percentage of the library's total spending on scientific and professional journals was dedicated to subscriptions with electronic access only? Broken out by full-time equivalent enrollment of the college.	173
Table 54.1.4	Approximately what percentage of the library's total spending on scientific and professional journals was dedicated to subscriptions with electronic access only? Broken out by public or private status of the college.	174
Table 54.1.5	Approximately what percentage of the library's total spending on scientific and professional journals was dedicated to subscriptions with electronic access only? Broken out by annual full-time tuition prior to any deductions.	174

Table 55	Approximately what percentage of the library's total spending on scientific and professional journals was dedicated to subscriptions with both print and electronic access?	175
Table 55.1.1	Approximately what percentage of the library's total spending on scientific and professional journals was dedicated to subscriptions with both print and electronic access?	175
Table 55.1.2	Approximately what percentage of the library's total spending on scientific and professional journals was dedicated to subscriptions with both print and electronic access? Broken out by type of college.	175
Table 55.1.3	Approximately what percentage of the library's total spending on scientific and professional journals was dedicated to subscriptions with both print and electronic access? Broken out by full-time equivalent enrollment of the college.	175
Table 55.1.4	Approximately what percentage of the library's total spending on scientific and professional journals was dedicated to subscriptions with both print and electronic access? Broken out by public or private status of the college.	176
Table 55.1.5	Approximately what percentage of the library's total spending on scientific and professional journals was dedicated to subscriptions with both print and electronic access? Broken out by annual full-time tuition prior to any deductions.	176
Table 56	What is the library's aggregated overall budget for its special collections division (or the departments that would fall under such a characterization)?	177
Table 56.1.1	What is the library's aggregated overall budget for its special collections division (or the departments that would fall under such a characterization)?	177
Table 56.1.2	What is the library's aggregated overall budget for its special collections division (or the departments that would fall under such a characterization)? Broken out by type of college.	177
Table 56.1.3	What is the library's aggregated overall budget for its special collections division (or the departments that would fall under such a characterization)? Broken out by full-time equivalent enrollment of the college.	177
Table 56.1.4	What is the library's aggregated overall budget for its special collections division (or the departments that would fall under such a characterization)? Broken out by public or private status of the college.	178
Table 56.1.5	What is the library's aggregated overall budget for its special collections division (or the departments that would fall under such a characterization)? Broken out by annual full-time tuition prior to any deductions.	178
Table 57	What was the percentage change in the library's total budget for special collections for the 2013-14 academic year?	179

Table 57.1.1   What was the percentage change in the library's total budget for special collections for the 2013-14 academic year? 179

Table 57.1.2   What was the percentage change in the library's total budget for special collections for the 2013-14 academic year? Broken out by type of college.. 179

Table 57.1.3   What was the percentage change in the library's total budget for special collections for the 2013-14 academic year? Broken out by full-time equivalent enrollment of the college. 179

Table 57.1.4   What was the percentage change in the library's total budget for special collections for the 2013-14 academic year? Broken out by public or private status of the college.. 180

Table 57.1.5   What was the percentage change in the library's total budget for special collections for the 2013-14 academic year? Broken out by annual full-time tuition prior to any deductions. 180

Table 58   What is the expected percentage change in the library's total budget for special collections for the 2014-15 academic year? 181

Table 58.1.1   What is the expected percentage change in the library's total budget for special collections for the 2014-15 academic year? 181

Table 59   How would you describe the digitization efforts of your special collections division?... 182

Table 59.1.1   How would you describe the digitization efforts of your special collections division?... 182

Table 59.1.2   How would you describe the digitization efforts of your special collections division? Broken out by type of college................................ 182

Table 59.1.3   How would you describe the digitization efforts of your special collections division? Broken out by full-time equivalent enrollment of the college.. 183

Table 59.1.4   How would you describe the digitization efforts of your special collections division? Broken out by public or private status of the college.. 183

Table 59.1.5   How would you describe the digitization efforts of your special collections division? Broken out by annual full-time tuition prior to any deductions... 183

Table 60   How would you characterize the library's attitude concerning the future of digitization of special collections at the library?............ 184

Table 60.1.1   How would you characterize the library's attitude concerning the future of digitization of special collections at the library?............ 184

Table 60.1.2   How would you characterize the library's attitude concerning the future of digitization of special collections at the library? Broken out by type of college... 184

Table 60.1.3   How would you characterize the library's attitude concerning the future of digitization of special collections at the library? Broken out by full-time equivalent enrollment of the college............. 185

Table 60.1.4   How would you characterize the library's attitude concerning the future of digitization of special collections at the library? Broken out by public or private status of the college............................ 185

Table 60.1.5	How would you characterize the library's attitude concerning the future of digitization of special collections at the library? Broken out by annual full-time tuition prior to any deductions.	186_Toc389570209
Table 61	What are the library's spending plans for video streaming in the next year?	187
Table 61.1.1	What are the library's spending plans for video streaming in the next year?	187
Table 61.1.2	What are the library's spending plans for video streaming in the next year? Broken out by type of college.	187
Table 61.1.3	What are the library's spending plans for video streaming in the next year? Broken out by full-time equivalent enrollment of the college.	188
Table 61.1.4	What are the library's spending plans for video streaming in the next year? Broken out by public or private status of the college.	188
Table 61.1.5	What are the library's spending plans for video streaming in the next year? Broken out by annual full-time tuition prior to any deductions.	188
Table 62	What are the library's spending plans for digital repository software and services in the next year?	189
Table 62.1.1	What are the library's spending plans for digital repository software and services in the next year?	189
Table 62.1.2	What are the library's spending plans for digital repository software and services in the next year? Broken out by type of college.	189
Table 62.1.3	What are the library's spending plans for digital repository software and services in the next year? Broken out by full-time equivalent enrollment of the college.	189
Table 62.1.4	What are the library's spending plans for digital repository software and services in the next year? Broken out by public or private status of the college.	190
Table 62.1.5	What are the library's spending plans for digital repository software and services in the next year? Broken out by annual full-time tuition prior to any deductions.	190
Table 63	What are the library's spending plans for cloud computing web storage devices in the next year?	191
Table 63.1.1	What are the library's spending plans for cloud computing web storage devices in the next year?	191
Table 63.1.2	What are the library's spending plans for cloud computing web storage devices in the next year? Broken out by type of college.	191
Table 63.1.3	What are the library's spending plans for cloud computing web storage devices in the next year? Broken out by full-time equivalent enrollment of the college.	191
Table 63.1.4	What are the library's spending plans for cloud computing web storage devices in the next year? Broken out by public or private status of the college.	192

Table 63.1.5   What are the library's spending plans for cloud computing web storage devices in the next year? Broken out by annual full-time tuition prior to any deductions.. 192

Table 64   What are the library's spending plans for RFID, barcoding, and other inventory-tracking technologies in the next year?...................... 193

Table 64.1.1   What are the library's spending plans for RFID, barcoding, and other inventory-tracking technologies in the next year?...................... 193

Table 64.1.2   What are the library's spending plans for RFID, barcoding, and other inventory-tracking technologies in the next year? Broken out by type of college.. 193

Table 64.1.3   What are the library's spending plans for RFID, barcoding, and other inventory-tracking technologies in the next year? Broken out by full-time equivalent enrollment of the college. 194

Table 64.1.4   What are the library's spending plans for RFID, barcoding, and other inventory-tracking technologies in the next year? Broken out by public or private status of the college... 194

Table 64.1.5   What are the library's spending plans for RFID, barcoding, and other inventory-tracking technologies in the next year? Broken out by annual full-time tuition prior to any deductions...................... 194

Table 65   What are the library's spending plans for book- or serials-binding technology and services in the next year?....................... 195

Table 65.1.1   What are the library's spending plans for book- or serials-binding technology and services in the next year?....................... 195

Table 65.1.2   What are the library's spending plans for book- or serials-binding technology and services in the next year? Broken out by type of college.. 195

Table 65.1.3   What are the library's spending plans for book- or serials-binding technology and services in the next year? Broken out by full-time equivalent enrollment of the college............................ 196

Table 65.1.4   What are the library's spending plans for book- or serials-binding technology and services in the next year? Broken out by public or private status of the college... 196

Table 65.1.5   What are the library's spending plans for book- or serials-binding technology and services in the next year? Broken out by annual full-time tuition prior to any deductions...................... 196

Table 66   What are the library's spending plans for artwork for the library in the next year?... 197

Table 66.1.1   What are the library's spending plans for artwork for the library in the next year?... 197

Table 66.1.2   What are the library's spending plans for artwork for the library in the next year? Broken out by type of college......................... 197

Table 66.1.3   What are the library's spending plans for artwork for the library in the next year? Broken out by full-time equivalent enrollment of the college.. 197

Table 66.1.4	What are the library's spending plans for artwork for the library in the next year? Broken out by public or private status of the college.	198
Table 66.1.5	What are the library's spending plans for artwork for the library in the next year? Broken out by annual full-time tuition prior to any deductions.	198
Table 67	What are the library's spending plans for whiteboards, classroom clickers, and other presentation/testing technologies in the next year?	199
Table 67.1.1	What are the library's spending plans for whiteboards, classroom clickers, and other presentation/testing technologies in the next year?	199
Table 67.1.2	What are the library's spending plans for whiteboards, classroom clickers, and other presentation/testing technologies in the next year? Broken out by type of college	199
Table 67.1.3	What are the library's spending plans for whiteboards, classroom clickers, and other presentation/testing technologies in the next year? Broken out by full-time equivalent enrollment of the college.	200
Table 67.1.4	What are the library's spending plans for whiteboards, classroom clickers, and other presentation/testing technologies in the next year? Broken out by public or private status of the college.	200
Table 67.1.5	What are the library's spending plans for whiteboards, classroom clickers, and other presentation/testing technologies in the next year? Broken out by annual full-time tuition prior to any deductions.	200
Table 68	What are the library's spending plans for mobile computing and telecommunications devices in the next year?	201
Table 68.1.1	What are the library's spending plans for mobile computing and telecommunications devices in the next year?	201
Table 68.1.2	What are the library's spending plans for mobile computing and telecommunications devices in the next year? Broken out by type of college.	201
Table 68.1.3	What are the library's spending plans for mobile computing and telecommunications devices in the next year? Broken out by full-time equivalent enrollment of the college.	201
Table 68.1.4	What are the library's spending plans for mobile computing and telecommunications devices in the next year? Broken out by public or private status of the college.	202
Table 68.1.5	What are the library's spending plans for mobile computing and telecommunications devices in the next year? Broken out by annual full-time tuition prior to any deductions.	202
Table 69	What are the library's spending plans for public relations or marketing services for the library in the next year?	203

Table 69.1.1	What are the library's spending plans for public relations or marketing services for the library in the next year?	203
Table 69.1.2	What are the library's spending plans for public relations or marketing services for the library in the next year? Broken out by type of college.	203
Table 69.1.3	What are the library's spending plans for public relations or marketing services for the library in the next year? Broken out by full-time equivalent enrollment of the college.	203
Table 69.1.4	What are the library's spending plans for public relations or marketing services for the library in the next year? Broken out by public or private status of the college.	204
Table 69.1.5	What are the library's spending plans for public relations or marketing services for the library in the next year? Broken out by annual full-time tuition prior to any deductions.	204
Table 70	What are the library's spending plans for applications software for media and computer centers or information commons in the next year?	205
Table 70.1.1	What are the library's spending plans for applications software for media and computer centers or information commons in the next year?	205
Table 70.1.2	What are the library's spending plans for applications software for media and computer centers or information commons in the next year? Broken out by type of college.	205
Table 70.1.3	What are the library's spending plans for applications software for media and computer centers or information commons in the next year? Broken out by full-time equivalent enrollment of the college.	206
Table 70.1.4	What are the library's spending plans for applications software for media and computer centers or information commons in the next year? Broken out by public or private status of the college.	206
Table 70.1.5	What are the library's spending plans for applications software for media and computer centers or information commons in the next year? Broken out by annual full-time tuition prior to any deductions.	206
Table 71	What are the library's spending plans for librarian travel and conferences in the next year?	207
Table 71.1.1	What are the library's spending plans for librarian travel and conferences in the next year?	207
Table 71.1.2	What are the library's spending plans for librarian travel and conferences in the next year? Broken out by type of college.	207
Table 71.1.3	What are the library's spending plans for librarian travel and conferences in the next year? Broken out by full-time equivalent enrollment of the college.	207

Table 71.1.4   What are the library's spending plans for librarian travel and conferences in the next year? Broken out by public or private status of the college. 208
Table 71.1.5   What are the library's spending plans for librarian travel and conferences in the next year? Broken out by annual full-time tuition prior to any deductions. 208
Table 72   What are the library's spending plans for librarian staff training in the next year? 209
Table 72.1.1   What are the library's spending plans for librarian staff training in the next year? 209
Table 72.1.2   What are the library's spending plans for librarian staff training in the next year? Broken out by type of college. 209
Table 72.1.3   What are the library's spending plans for librarian staff training in the next year? Broken out by full-time equivalent enrollment of the college. 209
Table 72.1.4   What are the library's spending plans for librarian staff training in the next year? Broken out by public or private status of the college. 210
Table 72.1.5   What are the library's spending plans for librarian staff training in the next year? Broken out by annual full-time tuition prior to any deductions. 210
Table 73   Does the library lend laptop computers to library patrons? 211
Table 73.1.1   Does the library lend laptop computers to library patrons? 211
Table 73.1.2   Does the library lend laptop computers to library patrons? Broken out by type of college. 211
Table 73.1.3   Does the library lend laptop computers to library patrons? Broken out by full-time equivalent enrollment of the college. 211
Table 73.1.4   Does the library lend laptop computers to library patrons? Broken out by public or private status of the college. 211
Table 73.1.5   Does the library lend laptop computers to library patrons? Broken out by annual full-time tuition prior to any deductions. 212
Table 74   Does the library lend tablet computers to library patrons? 213
Table 74.1.1   Does the library lend tablet computers to library patrons? 213
Table 74.1.2   Does the library lend tablet computers to library patrons? Broken out by type of college. 213
Table 74.1.3   Does the library lend tablet computers to library patrons? Broken out by full-time equivalent enrollment of the college. 213
Table 74.1.4   Does the library lend tablet computers to library patrons? Broken out by public or private status of the college. 213
Table 74.1.5   Does the library lend tablet computers to library patrons? Broken out by annual full-time tuition prior to any deductions. 214
Table 75   Does the library lend e-book reading devices to library patrons? 215
Table 75.1.1   Does the library lend e-book reading devices to library patrons? 215

Table 75.1.2	Does the library lend e-book reading devices to library patrons? Broken out by type of college.	215
Table 75.1.3	Does the library lend e-book reading devices to library patrons? Broken out by full-time equivalent enrollment of the college.	215
Table 75.1.4	Does the library lend e-book reading devices to library patrons? Broken out by public or private status of the college.	215
Table 75.1.5	Does the library lend e-book reading devices to library patrons? Broken out by annual full-time tuition prior to any deductions.	216
Table 76	If the library lends laptop computers to patrons, what is the total stock of devices available for loan?	217
Table 76.1.1	If the library lends laptop computers to patrons, what is the total stock of devices available for loan?	217
Table 76.1.2	If the library lends laptop computers to patrons, what is the total stock of devices available for loan? Broken out by type of college.	217
Table 76.1.3	If the library lends laptop computers to patrons, what is the total stock of devices available for loan? Broken out by full-time equivalent enrollment of the college.	217
Table 76.1.4	If the library lends laptop computers to patrons, what is the total stock of devices available for loan? Broken out by public or private status of the college.	218
Table 76.1.5	If the library lends laptop computers to patrons, what is the total stock of devices available for loan? Broken out by annual full-time tuition prior to any deductions.	218
Table 77	If the library lends tablet computers to patrons, what is the total stock of devices available for loan?	219
Table 77.1.1	If the library lends tablet computers to patrons, what is the total stock of devices available for loan?	219
Table 77.1.2	If the library lends tablet computers to patrons, what is the total stock of devices available for loan? Broken out by type of college.	219
Table 77.1.3	If the library lends tablet computers to patrons, what is the total stock of devices available for loan? Broken out by full-time equivalent enrollment of the college.	219
Table 77.1.4	If the library lends tablet computers to patrons, what is the total stock of devices available for loan? Broken out by public or private status of the college.	220
Table 77.1.5	If the library lends tablet computers to patrons, what is the total stock of devices available for loan? Broken out by annual full-time tuition prior to any deductions.	220
Table 78	If the library lends e-book reading devices to patrons, what is the total stock of devices available for loan?	221
Table 78.1.1	If the library lends e-book reading devices to patrons, what is the total stock of devices available for loan?	221

Table 78.1.2	If the library lends e-book reading devices to patrons, what is the total stock of devices available for loan? Broken out by type of college.	221
Table 78.1.3	If the library lends e-book reading devices to patrons, what is the total stock of devices available for loan? Broken out by full-time equivalent enrollment of the college.	221
Table 78.1.4	If the library lends e-book reading devices to patrons, what is the total stock of devices available for loan? Broken out by public or private status of the college.	222
Table 78.1.5	If the library lends e-book reading devices to patrons, what is the total stock of devices available for loan? Broken out by annual full-time tuition prior to any deductions.	222
Table 79	How much does the library plan to spend in the next year on laptop computers?	223
Table 79.1.1	How much does the library plan to spend in the next year on laptop computers?	223
Table 79.1.2	How much does the library plan to spend in the next year on laptop computers? Broken out by type of college.	223
Table 79.1.3	How much does the library plan to spend in the next year on laptop computers? Broken out by full-time equivalent enrollment of the college.	223
Table 79.1.4	How much does the library plan to spend in the next year on laptop computers? Broken out by public or private status of the college.	224
Table 79.1.5	How much does the library plan to spend in the next year on laptop computers? Broken out by annual full-time tuition prior to any deductions.	224
Table 80	How much does the library plan to spend in the next year on tablet computers?	225
Table 80.1.1	How much does the library plan to spend in the next year on tablet computers?	225
Table 80.1.2	How much does the library plan to spend in the next year on tablet computers? Broken out by type of college.	225
Table 80.1.3	How much does the library plan to spend in the next year on tablet computers? Broken out by full-time equivalent enrollment of the college.	225
Table 80.1.4	How much does the library plan to spend in the next year on tablet computers? Broken out by public or private status of the college.	226
Table 80.1.5	How much does the library plan to spend in the next year on tablet computers? Broken out by annual full-time tuition prior to any deductions.	226
Table 81	How much does the library plan to spend in the next year on e-book reading devices?	227
Table 81.1.1	How much does the library plan to spend in the next year on e-book reading devices?	227

Table 82	Does the library use any outsourced or cloud computing services on which to store metadata, files, special collections, or any other information?	228
Table 82.1.1	Does the library use any outsourced or cloud computing services on which to store metadata, files, special collections, or any other information?	228
Table 82.1.2	Does the library use any outsourced or cloud computing services on which to store metadata, files, special collections, or any other information? Broken out by type of college.	228
Table 82.1.3	Does the library use any outsourced or cloud computing services on which to store metadata, files, special collections, or any other information? Broken out by full-time equivalent enrollment of the college.	228
Table 82.1.4	Does the library use any outsourced or cloud computing services on which to store metadata, files, special collections, or any other information? Broken out by public or private status of the college.	228
Table 82.1.5	Does the library use any outsourced or cloud computing services on which to store metadata, files, special collections, or any other information? Broken out by annual full-time tuition prior to any deductions.	229

THE QUESTIONNAIRE

CHAPTER 1 – STAFF

1. What is the total staff of the library in terms of the number of full-time equivalent[1] positions?

2. What is the total annual cost of salaries, benefits, and other compensation for the library in the 2013-14 academic year?

3. Over the past year, how have the salaries and benefits for the librarians employed by your institution changed?

    A. More less declined
    B. Kept up with inflation
    C. Increased by less than 5%
    D. Increased by more than 5%

4. What was the total percentage change, if any, in the number of librarians[2] employed by your institution for the 2013-14 academic year?

CHAPTER 2 – STUDENT WORKERS

5. How many students work in your library?

6. What is the average number of hours worked per week for the students who work in your library?

7. What is the average hourly rate of pay (in USD) for the students who work in your library?

8. Describe the library training, if any, your student workers receive.

CHAPTER 3 – CHANGES IN THE DEPLOYMENT OF LABOR

9. Describe any significant changes in the way the library has deployed labor in the past few years (or any upcoming plans for changes). Have you increased (or plan to increase) the number of full- or part-time positions in a given division? Have you been able to increase productivity in a division and make do with less labor?

---

[1] Includes full-time equivalent of all personnel (technical, clerical, professional, etc.)
[2] Not support staff

10. As a general rule, how do you expect resource allocation to the library over the next few years to stack up vis-à-vis other academic departments in your institution?

    A. We expect to do better than other departments
    B. We expect to keep pace with other departments
    C. We expect to do worse than other departments

CHAPTER 4 – MATERIALS & A/V SPENDING

11. What is the library's total spending on materials/content[1] for the 2013-14 academic year?

12. By how much did materials spending change (not accounting for inflation) in the 2013-14 academic year?

13. By how much do you expect materials spending to change in the 2014-15 academic year?

14. How much will the library spend of information accessed online in the 2013-14 academic year?

15. What was the rate of change in the library's spending on online content/information between the 2012-13 and 2013-14 academic years?

16. Over the past two years, how has the library's spending on video resources such as films, DVDs, film downloads via the web, and other video-streaming technologies changed?

    A. Declined
    B. Remained the same
    C. Increased by less than 5%
    D. Increased by more than 5%

17. What was the library's spending on audio-visual resources in the 2013-14 academic year?

18. What do you expect the library's spending on audio-visual resources to be in the 2014-15 academic year?

---

[1] Includes books, e-books, online databases, CD-ROM/DVD/tape databases, audio-visual resources, journals, magazines, directories, and other periodicals

CHAPTER 5 – GRANTS

19. Has the library received any grant support in the past year from _____?

    A. Federal agencies
    B. State or local government agencies
    C. Foundations
    D. Private companies
    E. Special funds of the university
    F. Alumni

20. What was the total value of spending derived from grants in the 2012-13 academic year?

21. What do you expect will be the total value of spending derived from grants in the 2013-14 academic year?

22. How much did the library accrue from special endowments in the past year?

CHAPTER 6 – CAPITAL SPENDING

23. In the past two years, how has the library's capital budget changed?

    A. Decreased
    B. Remained the same
    C. Increased somewhat
    D. Increased significantly

24. Over the next three years, how do you expect the library's capital budget to change?

    A. Decrease
    B. Remain the same
    C. Increase somewhat
    D. Increase significantly

25. How has capital spending[1] on _____ changed over the past three years?

    A. New library buildings
    B. Extensions or significant renovations of existing library buildings
    C. Repairs to library buildings
    D. Maintenance of IT equipment stock

---

[1] If spending has been impacted by funds from another source (e.g. grants, special legislative earmarks, and donations or other sources that are not part of the capital budget), you should consider this as part of the capital budget for the purposes of this question

E.   New IT equipment

CHAPTER 7 – TECHNOLOGY EDUCATION CENTER

26. How much has the library spent over the past three years to develop new library instructional centers or to re-equip/upgrade existing ones with new computers, workstations, or other technology?

27. If your library plays a role in the student retention efforts of your college, explain this role, including what services, technologies, and approaches you have found effective, as well as your plans for the future.

CHAPTER 8 – BOOKS

28. How much did the library spend on traditional print books in the 2013-14 academic year?

29. How much do you expect the library to spend on print books in the 2014-15 academic year?

30. How much did the library spend on subscribing to or purchasing e-books in the _____ academic year?

    A.   2012-13
    B.   2013-14

31. How much do you expect the library to spend on subscribing to or purchasing e-books in the 2014-15 academic year?

32. What was the library's total spending on books or other intellectual property with _____ in the 2012-13 academic year?

    A.   Amazon
    B.   Alibris
    C.   Barnes & Noble
    D.   Powell's Books
    E.   Books-A-Million
    F.   All other online booksellers

33. What was the library's total spending (including all online booksellers) on books or other intellectual property in the 2012-13 academic year?

34. Has the library purchased e-book readers, iPads, or any other devices for patrons to read e-books?

The Survey of Academic Libraries, 2014-15 Edition

35. Over the past two years, how much has the library spent on _____?

   A. E-book readers and devices
   B. Books and other content for e-book readers and devices
   C. Software to e-book enable computers or mobile devices

CHAPTER 9 – JOURNALS

36. How much did the library spend on print and electronic subscriptions to scholarly and professional journals in the _____ academic year?

   A. 2012-13
   B. 2013-14
   C. 2014-15 (anticipated)

37. Approximately what percentage of the library's total spending on scientific and professional journals was dedicated to _____?

   A. Print subscriptions only
   B. Subscriptions with electronic access only
   C. Subscriptions with both print and electronic access

CHAPTER 10 – SPECIAL COLLECTIONS

38. What is the library's aggregated overall budget for its special collections division (or the departments that would fall under such a characterization)?

39. What was the percentage change in the library's total budget for special collections for the 2013-14 academic year?

40. What is the expected percentage change in the library's total budget for special collections for the 2014-15 academic year?

41. How would you describe the digitization efforts of your special collections division?

   A. We don't have special collections
   B. Have not digitized much
   C. Have digitized small-scale projects
   D. Have made a significant effort to digitize

42. How would you characterize the library's attitude concerning the future of digitization of special collections at the library?

   A. Won't be doing much of this in the future

B. Definitely in the plans, but we are just getting started
C. Plans have been approved for significant investments
D. Plan on making a major push to digitize appropriate segments

CHAPTER 11 – SPENDING TRENDS

43. What are the library's spending plans for _____ in the next year?

   A. Video streaming
   B. Digital repository software and services
   C. Cloud computing web storage services
   D. RFID, barcoding, and other inventory-tracking technologies
   E. Book- or serials-binding technology and services
   F. Artwork for the library
   G. Whiteboards, classroom clickers, and other presentation/testing technologies
   H. Mobile computing and telecommunications devices
   I. Public relations or marketing services for the library
   J. Applications software for media and computer centers or information commons
   K. Librarian travel and conferences
   L. Librarian staff training

CHAPTER 12 – COMPUTING DEVICES AND LIBRARY INFORMATION TECHNOLOGY

44. Does the library lend _____ to library patrons?

   A. Laptop computers
   B. Tablet computers
   C. E-book reading devices

45. If the library lends _____ to patrons, what is the total stock of devices available for loan?

   A. Laptop computers
   B. Tablet computers
   C. E-book reading devices

46. How much does the library plan to spend in the next year on _____?

   A. Laptop computers
   B. Tablet computers
   C. E-book reading devices

47. Does the library use any outsourced or cloud computing services on which to store metadata, files, special collections, or any other information?

SURVEY PARTICIPANTS

Angelina College
Cincinnati State Technical and Community College
Coastal Carolina University
Eckerd College
Emporia State University
Florida Keys Community College
Gogebic Community College
Gulf Coast State College
Institute Superior de Agronomia-Universidade de Lisboa
Jackson State Community College
Johnson County Community College
Lawrence Technological University
Limestone College
London Metropolitan University
Mercer County Community College
Mott Community College
Muscatine Community College
Pfeiffer University
Quinnipiac University
South Arkansas Community College
South Dakota State University
Southern Polytechnic State University
University of Chichester
University of Tsukuba

CHARACTERISTICS OF THE SAMPLE

Overall sample size: 24

By Type of College
Community college	11
4-year BA- or MA-granting college	6
PhD-granting college or research university	7

By Full-Time Enrollment
Less than 2,500	8
2,500 to 7,499	9
7,500 or more	7

By Public or Private Status
Public	19
Private	5

By Annual Full-Time Tuition
Less than $5,000	10
$5,000 to $14,999	7
$15,000 or more	7

Type of college, broken out by full-time equivalent enrollment of the college.

Type of College	Less than 2,500	2,500 to 7,499	7,500 or more
Community college	36.36%	45.45%	18.18%
4-year BA- or MA- granting college	50.00%	33.33%	16.67%
PhD-granting college or research university	14.29%	28.57%	57.14%

Type of college, broken out by public or private status of the college.

Type of College	Public	Private
Community college	100.00%	0.00%
4-year BA- or MA-granting college	50.00%	50.00%
PhD-granting college or research university	71.43%	28.57%

Type of college, broken out by annual full-time tuition prior to any deductions.

Type of College	Less than $5,000	$5,000 to $14,999	$15,000 or more
Community college	72.73%	27.27%	0.00%
4-year BA- or MA- granting college	16.67%	33.33%	50.00%
PhD-granting college or research university	14.29%	28.57%	57.14%

Full-time equivalent enrollment of the college, broken out by type of college.

Enrollment	Community college	4-year BA- or MA- granting college	PhD-granting college or research university
Less than 2,500	50.00%	37.50%	12.50%
2,500 to 7,499	55.56%	22.22%	22.22%
7,500 or more	28.57%	14.29%	57.14%

Full-time equivalent enrollment of the college, broken out by public or private status of the college.

Enrollment	Public	Private
Less than 2,500	62.50%	37.50%
2,500 to 7,499	88.89%	11.11%
7,500 or more	85.71%	14.29%

Full-time equivalent enrollment of the college, broken out by annual full-time tuition prior to any deductions.

Enrollment	Less than $5,000	$5,000 to $14,999	$15,000 or more
Less than 2,500	50.00%	12.50%	37.50%
2,500 to 7,499	44.44%	44.44%	11.11%
7,500 or more	28.57%	28.57%	42.86%

Public or private status of the college, broken out by type of college.

Public or Private	Community college	4-year BA- or MA- granting college	PhD-granting college or research university
Public	57.89%	15.79%	26.32%
Private	0.00%	60.00%	40.00%

Public or private status of the college, broken out by full-time equivalent enrollment of the college.

Public or Private	Less than 2,500	2,500 to 7,499	7,500 or more
Public	26.32%	42.11%	31.58%
Private	60.00%	20.00%	20.00%

Public or private status of the college, broken out by annual full-time tuition prior to any deductions.

Public or Private	Less than $5,000	$5,000 to $14,999	$15,000 or more
Public	52.63%	36.84%	10.53%
Private	0.00%	0.00%	100.00%

Annual full-time tuition prior to any deductions, broken out by type of college.

Tuition	Community college	4-year BA- or MA- granting college	PhD-granting college or research university
Less than $5,000	80.00%	10.00%	10.00%
$5,000 to $14,999	42.86%	28.57%	28.57%
$15,000 or more	0.00%	42.86%	57.14%

Annual full-time tuition prior to any deductions, broken out by full-time equivalent enrollment of the college.

Tuition	Less than 2,500	2,500 to 7,499	7,500 or more
Less than $5,000	40.00%	40.00%	20.00%
$5,000 to $14,999	14.29%	57.14%	28.57%
$15,000 or more	42.86%	14.29%	42.86%

Annual full-time tuition prior to any deductions, broken out by public or private status of the college.

Tuition	Public	Private
Less than $5,000	100.00%	0.00%
$5,000 to $14,999	100.00%	0.00%
$15,000 or more	28.57%	71.43%

SUMMARY OF MAIN FINDINGS

CHAPTER 1 – STAFF

Full-Time Equivalent Staff

Survey participants have an average of 16.38 full-time equivalent staff positions at the library. The overall sample median, however, is 10, with the range being from 1.8 to 80. Only a quarter (6 of 24) of all participants have at least 15 FTE positions (all of which are public schools with an enrollment of at least 2,500), while more than half (13 of 24) have 10 FTE or fewer. The PhD-granting colleges and research universities in the sample have the highest mean here (28.36 FTE), while the community colleges have the lowest (8.79 FTE). Only two participants have more than 33 FTE (52 and 80, respectively), both of which are public PhD-granting colleges or research universities with at least 7,500 students. Public schools have nearly twice the mean of the private schools in the sample, 18.17 and 9.58, respectively. Those participants with higher annual tuitions tend to have more FTE positions on the library staff, as the mean for the lowest tuition range (less than $5,000) is less than half that of the other two means at 8.62 FTE.

Annual Cost of Salaries

The mean annual cost of salaries, benefits, and other compensations for the libraries in the sample in the 2013-14 academic year is $662,330. However, this is greatly offset by a few larger responses as the median is nearly half that figure at $361,000. Just 4 of 20 respondents reported over $650,000 in total salaries, with the top spot belonging to a PhD-granting college or research university at $3.3 million. 8 of 20 respondents put this figure at $200,000 or less. Understandably, participants with the highest enrollments generally have larger costs of salaries (a mean of $1.84 million) as these libraries tend to have greater numbers of FTE staff—by comparison, those participants in the middle enrollment range (2,500 to 7,499) have a mean total cost of salaries of $529,546, and those in the lowest enrollment range (less than 2,500) have a mean of just $203,982. Likewise, survey participants with higher annual tuitions have higher total annual costs of salaries.

Change in Salaries

An overwhelming majority of survey participants (70.83 percent) report that librarian salaries and benefits have, over the past year, more or less declined. Just 16.67 percent say they have kept up with inflation, while the remaining 12.5 percent say they have increased by less than 5 percent (no participant say salaries have increased by more than 5 percent). The only colleges to report any sort of increase in this sense are the four-year BA- or MA-granting colleges, while 81.82 percent of community colleges say salaries have declined. Those schools with the highest annual tuition ($15,000 or more) are the most positive here, as just 42.86 percent of them say salaries have declined, while at least 80 percent of all other participants can say the same.

Change in Number of Librarians

For the 2013-14 academic year, 17 of 24 survey participants did not report any change in the number of librarians employed by their respective institutions. Just two participants reported an increased in this number (of 1 and 2 percent, respectively) and five participants reported a decrease (with one participant reporting a decrease of as much as 25 percent), resulting in an overall sample mean of a 2.88 percent decrease. Broken out by type of college, all means fell between a decrease of 2.33 percent and a decrease of 4 percent. In fact, the mean for every breakout for this question fell in a similar range: between a decrease of 1.89 percent and a decrease of 4.14 percent. This is largely the work of four participants that reported decreases between 10 and 25 percent, as the remaining 20 participants in the sample all fell between a 2 percent decrease and a 2 percent increase.

CHAPTER 2 – STUDENT WORKERS

Number of Student Workers

The libraries in the sample each employ a mean of 11.2 student workers. The median is 7, and the range is from 0 to 80, although just the one library out of 23 respondents has more than 24 student workers. No community college has more than 8 student workers, resulting in a mean of 3.5, while the PhD-granting colleges and research universities (mean of 11.14) and four-year BA- or MA-granting colleges (mean of 24.08) have significantly higher numbers. While the split between public (mean of 11.28) and private (mean of 10.9) is nearly negligible, there appears a reliable correlation when the data is broken out by total enrollment: those participants with enrollments under 2,500 have a mean of just 4.94 student workers, which increases slightly to a mean of 7.67 for the next enrollment range (2,500 to 7,499) before more than tripling to a mean of 24.83 for the top enrollment range (7,500 or more). Likewise, those libraries with an annual tuition under $5,000 have a mean of just 3.22 student workers (and a median of 2).

Hours Worked Per Week

These students work a mean of 11.25 total hours per week in the library. The range is from 5 to 20 hours. Interestingly, while the community colleges in the sample have the least number of student workers, their students put in the most hours, a mean of 14.28 hours per work. The four-year BA- or MA-granting colleges report a mean of 12.58 hours/week, while the PhD-granting colleges and research universities have a mean of just 10.33 hours/week. Public schools (mean of 13.22) maintain a slight edge over the private schools (mean of 10.9). As annual tuition increases, the number of hours worked by these student workers in the library steadily decreases: those participants in the lowest tuition range (less than $5,000) report a mean of 14.64 hours/week worked, a figure which drops to 12.71 for the middle range ($5,000 to $14,999) and then down to 10.64 for the top range ($15,000 or more).

Hourly Wage

Student workers earn a mean of $8.71/hour. While the overall sample range is from $5.15/hour to $21.34/hour, 18 of 20 respondents all fall within the range of $7.25/hour and $12.70/hour (and 14 of those participants are between $7.25 and $8.00). The overall sample median is $7.85/hour, and all medians for all breakouts for this question fall between $7.48/hour and $8.50/hour. Those participants with higher tuitions tend to provide higher hourly wages for their student workers: those in the lowest tuition range have a mean hourly wage of $7.69/hour, which jumps to $8.58/hour for the middle tuition range before topping out at $10.06/hour for the highest tuition level—the last of which includes one participant's response of $21.34/hour.

CHAPTER 3 – CHANGES IN THE DEPLOYMENT OF LABOR

Library Resource Allocation Compared to Other Academic Departments

We asked survey participants how they expect the library to stack up in terms of resource allocation over the next few years relative to other academic departments. Just one participant (4.17 percent) expects the library to do better than other departments. The remaining participants are nearly evenly split: 12 libraries (50 percent) expect to "keep pace with other departments," while 11 libraries (45.83 percent) expect to "do worse than other departments." Most of those participants that expect to keep pace are either four-year BA- or MA-granting colleges or else PhD-granting colleges and research universities, as only 36.36 percent of community colleges can say the same. Furthermore, of the 12 participants that expect to keep pace, 8 are in the middle enrollment range (2,500 to 7,499 students). Exactly 57.14 percent of all participants with annual tuitions of at least $5,000 expect to keep pace, as compared to just 40 percent of those with tuitions under $5,000.

CHAPTER 4 – MATERIALS & A/V SPENDING

Total Spending on Materials/Content in 2013-14

For the 2013-14 academic year, libraries in the sample spent a mean of $628,274 on materials and content (this includes spending on books, e-books, online databases, CD-Rom/DVD/tape databases, audio-visual resources, journals, magazines, directories, and other periodicals). This mean, however, is greatly offset by a handful of larger responses, as the overall sample median is just $120,000. While the range is from $20,425 to $5 million, 18 of 21 respondents spent less than $1 million, with nearly half of them spending less than $100,000. The three participants that spent more than $1 million are all PhD-granting colleges or research universities, resulting in a mean of $1.64 million for this category (and a median of $967,500). By comparison, community colleges in the sample spent a mean of just $116,111 on content and materials (and a median of $58.030). As could be expected, spending increases dramatically as both enrollment and tuition increase.

Rate of Change in Spending

Spending on materials and content didn't change much for the 2013-14 academic year, as libraries in the sample reported a mean increase of just 0.38 percent for this time period. 12 of 23 respondents reported no change at all, and another five participants report a range between a 5 percent decrease and 5 percent increase. One participant reported a 30 percent decrease, while two other participants reported 30 percent increases, all three of which are community colleges with an annual tuition under $15,000. The median for every breakout category for this question is 0 percent (no change).

These figures are not expected to change much for the 2014-15 academic year, as the libraries in the sample expect a mean increase of just 0.23 percent. The relationships that emerged for the 2013-14 academic year are expected to uphold for the 2014-15 academic year.

Spending on Information Accessed Online

The libraries in the sample spent a mean of $305,560 on information accessed online in the 2013-14 academic year. The median, however, was $60,000, and the range was from a minimum of $6,000 to a maximum of $2.15 million. Community colleges spent by far the least here, with a mean of $73,109 and a median of $33,000, while the PhD-granting colleges and research universities spent the most, a mean of $708,901 and a median of $335,000—which includes the two participants that spent over $1 million to this end. As enrollment increases, so too does spending on information accessed online: those participants in the lowest enrollment range (less than 2,500) spent a mean of just $92,720, a figure which rises to $127,541 for the middle range (2,500 to 7,499) and then increases exponentially to a mean of $797,033 for the top range (7,500 or more). A similar relationship exists when the data is broken out by annual tuition.

Rate of Change in Spending on Online Content/Information

Between the 2012-13 and 2013-14 academic years, the libraries in the sample increased spending on online content/information by a mean of 3.95 percent. Just one participant reported a decrease in spending here (a decrease of 20 percent), and exactly half (11 of 22) of all respondents reported an increase, with three participants reporting an increase between 20 and 24 percent. The remaining 10 respondents reported no change.

Change in Spending on Video Resources

37.5 percent of all libraries in the sample report that spending on video resources such as films, DVDs, film downloads via the web, and other video-streaming technologies has declined over the past two years, while another 37.5 percent say it has remained the same. The remaining quarter of participants are split evenly between an increase of less than 5 percent and an increase of more than 5 percent—none of which are PhD-granting colleges or research universities.

Spending on A/V Resources in 2013-14

The libraries in the sample spent a mean of $9,231 on audio-visual resources in the 2013-14 academic year. While a handful of participants spent between $15,000 and $40,000 (all of which are public schools), the overall sample median was $4,000 as 10 of 18 respondents spent $5,000 or less. There is a clear correlation between enrollment and the amount of spending here: libraries with less than 2,500 students spent a mean of just $2,782, while those with at least 7,500 students spent a mean of $23,800 on A/V resources during this time. The same relationship does not hold true when the data is broken out by annual tuition, however, as those libraries in the highest tuition range ($15,000 or more) spent the least on A/V resources, a mean of just $3,411, with no participant here spending more than $8,254 in this respect.

For the 2014-15 academic year, the libraries in the sample expect only slight variations from the 2013-14 spending figures (the overall sample mean will drop slightly to $8,789).

CHAPTER 5 – GRANTS

Sources of Grant Support

We asked our survey participants if they had received any grant support in the past year from any of the following sources: federal agencies; state or local government agencies; foundations; private companies; special funds of the university; or alumni. No libraries received any grant support from private companies, and just one participant each received grant support from special funds of the university or from alumni. Two participants each received funding from federal agencies or from foundations, all four of which are public schools with annual tuitions under $15,000. With three participants reporting they have received grant support in the past year from state or local government agencies, this source proved to be (albeit by matter of scale) the most popular among our survey participants.

Total Spending from Grants

For the 2012-13 academic year, libraries in the sample estimated the total value of spending derived from grants to be a mean of $1,385. However, 14 of 20 respondents put this figure at $0, with just one of the remaining six participants valuing this over $5,000. The median for every breakout category in this question is $0, with one exception: among those four-year BA- or MA-granting colleges in the sample, the mean was $4,250 and the median was $2,500.

For spending derived from grants in the 2013-14 academic year, the one participant with the response of $12,000 in the previous year expects this figure to be $0, bringing the overall sample maximum down to $5,000 and resulting in an overall sample mean of just $665.

Money from Special Endowments

The libraries in the sample accrued a mean of $2,266 from special endowments in the past year. However, 14 of 19 respondents did not accrue anything from special endowments, and among those participants that did accrue any money, just two put this figure higher than $500 (at $2,000 and $40,000, respectively). Both of these participants have an annual tuition of at least $15,000. The one participant that accrued $40,000 from special endowments is a private four-year BA- or MA-granting college with an enrollment under 2,500.

CHAPTER 6 – CAPITAL SPENDING

Change in the Library's Capital Budget

For nearly half (45.83 percent) of all survey participants, the library's capital budget has declined over the past two years. 37.5 percent of participants report that it has remained the same, leaving just three participants (12.5 percent) to report that it has "increased somewhat" and one participant (4.17 percent) who says it has "increased significantly." Broken out by full-time equivalent enrollment, 85.71 percent of participants with 7,500 or more students have seen the library's capital budget decline over this time, while 62.5 percent of those participants with enrollments under 2,500 report that it has remained the same. There appears a clear relationship between the capital budget and the institution's annual tuition: while 60 percent of those participants in the lowest tuition range (less than $5,000) have seen this decline, this figure drops to 42.86 percent for the middle range ($5,000 to $14,999) and then down again to 28.57 percent for the top range ($15,000 or more).

The libraries in the sample are just as pessimistic concerning the fate of the library's capital budget over the next three years, with 58.33 percent of them saying it will decline over this time and a third saying it will remain the same. Just the two remaining participants (8.33 percent) believe it will "increase somewhat." Similarly, those participants with higher tuitions are a bit more optimistic, as 57.14 percent of those in the $15,000 or more range believe the library's budget will remain the same, while at least 70 percent of all other participants believe the budget will decline over this time.

CHAPTER 7 – TECHNOLOGY EDUCATION CENTER

Spending on Developing New Library Instructional Centers

The libraries in the sample spent a mean of $340,785 over the past three years to develop new library instructional centers or to re-equip/upgrade existing ones with new computers, workstations, or other technologies. However, this mean is greatly offset by one participant's response of $6.69 million, the only participant to spend more than $50,000 (and just one of eight participants who had spent anything at all), resulting in an overall sample median of $0. This one participant is a public PhD-granting college or research university with an annual tuition between $5,000 and $15,000. No private schools in the sample spent more than $5,000 in this respect, nor did any participant with an annual tuition of at least $15,000.

CHAPTER 8 – BOOKS

Spending on Traditional Print Books

In the 2013-14 academic year, the libraries in the sample spent a mean of $82,343 on traditional print books. The range is from a minimum of $2,700 to a maximum of $439,551. PhD-granting colleges and research universities spent the most on print books, spending a mean of $201,450 in 2013-14, while the community colleges in the sample spent a mean of just $32,464 in that same time. Increased enrollment seems to ensure increased spending on print books: those participants with less than 2,500 students spent a mean of $26,709 on this, a figure which more than doubles to $65,857 for the middle enrollment range (2,500 to 7,499) before nearly tripling to $194,439 for the top enrollment group (7,500 or more). A similar trend occurs when the data is broken out by annual tuition, culminating with a mean spending of $159,087 among those participants in the top tuition range ($15,000 or more).

Spending on traditional print books is expected to dip slightly for the 2014-15 academic, dropping to an overall sample mean of $77,768. 9 of 20 respondents expect their spending to decline from the year before, 8 participants expect it to remain the same, and just 3 participants believe it will increase. Still, the PhD-granting colleges and research universities expect to spend the most (a mean of $186,671), and increasing enrollments and tuitions signal increased spending for participants in this area.

Spending on E-Books

In the 2012-13 academic year, libraries in the sample spent a mean of $9,696 subscribing to or purchasing e-books. The median is $3,750, and the range is from $0 to $40,542. Broken out by type of college, the biggest spenders here are the four-year BA- or MA-granting colleges, which spent a mean of $25,136 in 2012-13 in this manner, while the community colleges spent a mean of just $4,400 and the PhD-granting colleges and research universities a mean of just $5,000. A similar discrepancy arises when the data is broken out by full-time enrollment: those participants with 7,500 or more students spent a mean of $21,667 on e-books, a figure which drops to $4,500 for the middle enrollment range (2,500 to 7,499) and $8,455 for the lowest range (less than 2,500). However, as annual tuition increases, so too does spending on e-books, from a mean of $3,586 for the lowest tuition range (less than $5,000) up to a mean of $15,108 for the top range ($15,000 or more).

Overall spending increased in the 2013-14 academic year, to a mean of $11,766, and is only expected to increase again for the 2014-15 academic year to a mean of $14,844. Spending trends unveiled in the 2012-13 academic year are mirrored in the 2013-14 year and are expected to continue in this same fashion for the 2014-15 academic year.

Spending on Online Booksellers

We asked our survey participants how much the library spent in the 2012-13 academic year on books or other intellectual property on the following online booksellers: Amazon; Alibris; Barnes & Noble; Powell's Books; and Books-A-Million. Of these five, Amazon was the clear favorite, with participants spending a mean of $9,061 through the online seller. The range is from $0 to $50,000, and the median is $3,000. On average, the four-year BA- or MA-granting colleges in the sample spent more than twice as much as the community colleges, with means of $13,333 and $6,011, respectively. Predictably, increased enrollments and tuitions led to increased spending on Amazon. Those participants in the highest tuition bracket ($15,000 or more) spent, on average, nearly twice as much as those participants in the middle tuition range ($5,000 to $14,999), with a mean of $13,767 for the former and a mean of $7,625. An even bigger gap occurs when the data is broken out by enrollment: while those participants with 7,500 or more students spent a mean of $26,459 in this respect, no other breakout in this category posted a mean higher than $3,250.

Participants spent a mean of $5,017 on Alibris and a mean of $5,073 on Barnes & Noble. However, mean spending on the former was greatly affected by one participant's response of $75,000 (a public PhD-granting college or research university with at least 7,500 students and annual tuition of at least $15,000), and in fact just one other participant had spent anything at all on Alibris, and that a meager $250. Spending at Barnes & Noble was barely more varied, as two participants spent $20,000 and $56,000, respectively, and a third participant had spent $100, constituting all spending for the entire sample.

No participants spent anything at all on Books-A-Million, and just one participant spent $200 at Powell's Books, resulting in an overall sample mean of just $13.33.

Total Spending on Books and All Other Intellectual Property

For the 2012-13 academic year, the libraries in the sample spent a mean of $36,886 on books and all other intellectual property. The range is from $0 to $300,000, although just the one library out of 15 respondents spent more than $75,000. As is consistent with the spending breakdown by online booksellers, the PhD-granting colleges and research universities outspent all other types of colleges in the sample, posting a mean of $63,107. While the next closest mean belongs to the four-year BA- and MA-granting colleges ($38,333), the medians greatly favor this second group over the PhD-granting colleges and research universities, $25,000 to $2,700, respectively. Broken out by enrollment, however, the participants in the top range (7,500 or more) posted a mean of $106,459, more than seven times that of the next closest mean in this category. What's more, these same participants compiled a median of $62,500, or more than 12 times that of the next closest median.

Purchasing iPads and Other E-book Readers

A third of all survey participants have purchased iPads or other such devices in order for their patrons to read e-books. This practice is most common among the four-year BA- or MA-granting colleges, as half of them made such purchases, compared to just 27.27 percent of community colleges and 28.57 percent of PhD-granting colleges and research universities in the sample. As enrollment increases, so too does the likelihood of the library purchasing e-book readers for its patrons: while only 25 percent of those in the bottom enrollment range (less than 2,500 students) have done so, this figure increases to 33.33 percent for the middle range (2,500 to 7,499) and up again to 42.86 percent for the top range (7,500 or more).

Spending on E-Book Readers and Devices, E-Books and Content, and Software

Over the past two years, the libraries in the sample have spent a mean of just $160.53 on e-book readers and devices. 14 of 19 respondents did not spend anything over this time period, while the remaining five participants spent the following amounts: $300; $350; $400; $1,000; and $1,000. Both participants that spent $1,000 are community colleges with at least 2,500 students and an annual tuition under $15,000.

Likewise, while the libraries in the sample spent a mean of $856.58 on books and other content for e-book readers and devices over the past two years, this figure is greatly offset by one participant's response of $15,000. Of the remaining 18 respondents, just three spent anything at all: $75; $200; and $1,000. The participant that spent $15,000 here is a PhD-granting college or research university in both the top enrollment and tuition range in our sample.

No library in the sample has spent any money in the last two years on e-book-enabling software.

CHAPTER 9 – JOURNALS

Spending on Journal Subscriptions

The libraries in the sample spent a mean of $341,186 in the 2012-13 academic year on print and electronic subscriptions to scholarly and professional journals. The median is $42,000, and the range is from $800 to $3 million. Broken out by type of college, the PhD-granting colleges and research universities are the big spenders here, spending a mean of $936,988 (this includes the $3 million) and a median of $631,852. By comparison, no other participant in the survey spent more than $517,698, resulting in means of $189,425 and $11,435 for the four-year BA-/MA-granting colleges and community colleges, respectively. Of the 19 respondents, 7 libraries spent at least $100,000 on journals, while 8 libraries spent $8,000 or less. The bigger institutions proved to be bigger spenders, as those participants with at least 7,500 students spent a mean of $1.08 million on print and electronic journal subscriptions, while those in the middle enrollment range (2,500 to 7,499) spent a mean of just $71,138. A large gap occurs when the data is broken out by annual tuition: while those participants with an annual tuition of at least $5,000 spent a mean of at least $515,234 to this end, those institutions with tuitions below $5,000 spent a mean of just $9,616.

Spending increased slightly in 2013-14, as just 5 respondents reported a decrease in spending from the previous year, 10 respondents reported an increase, and 4 libraries did not see a change in spending at all. The overall mean rose to $359,192. A similar bump is expected for the 2014-15 academic year: 10 participants anticipate an increase in spending, 4 expect spending to decline, and 5 libraries do not expect any changes in this regard. Overall mean spending in 2014-15 is expected to reach $379,854.

Spending on Print and Electronic Journals by Percentage

We asked our survey participants to estimate how the library's total spending on scientific and professional journals was divided into three areas: print subscriptions only; electronic subscriptions only; and subscriptions with both print and electronic access. The libraries in the sample estimate that a mean of 43.96 percent of their total spending is dedicated to subscriptions with electronic access only. A mean of 34.11 percent is dedicated to print subscriptions, while a mean of 21.93 percent goes toward subscriptions with both print and electronic access. Among some peculiarities in the data, the community colleges in the sample estimate a mean of 48.75 percent of spending is dedicated to print subscriptions only, nearly 15 percentage points over the overall sample mean. As annual tuition increases, libraries become less likely to dedicate large amounts of spending to print-only subscriptions: while respondents in the lowest tuition bracket estimate that a shade more than half (51.05 percent) of the library's spending goes to print subscriptions, this figure drops way down to 15.17 percent for the top tuition bracket ($15,000 or more). When considering electronic-only subscriptions, the opposite holds true, as those participants in the top tuition bracket estimate a mean 68.73 percent of total spending is allocated in this way, compared to a mean of just 23.95 percent for those in the bottom bracket. The four-year BA- or MA- granting colleges are the biggest proponents here, as these participants estimate a mean of 66.54 percent of their overall spending is dedicated to electronic-only subscriptions.

CHAPTER 10 – SPECIAL COLLECTIONS

Special Collections Budget

Very few participants have any sort of budget for its special collections division or department. Of the 16 respondents, just four report anything other than $0, with the maximum being $5,000. This results in an overall sample mean of $541.88. Three of these four respondents (those libraries with the highest special collections budgets) each have an annual tuition of at least $15,000.

Just two participants reported any change in the library's total budget for special collections for the 2013-14 academic year. The first, a community college in both the middle enrollment and tuition range, reported a 100 percent increase. The second, a PhD-granting college or research university in both the top enrollment tuition range, reported a 90 percent decrease in the special collections budget. No library in the sample expects any change in this budget for the 2014-15 academic year.

Current Digitization Efforts of Special Collections

We asked survey participants to describe the digitization efforts of their library's special collections division. While 20.83 percent of libraries in the sample do not have a special collections department, 41.67 percent of participants say this department has completed small-scale digitization projects. Just 8.33 percent say special collections has made a significant effort to digitize, while the remaining 29.17 percent admit the department has not digitized much. The four-year BA- and MA-granting colleges are perhaps the most active here, as 83.33 percent of them report that special collections has digitized small-scale projects. On the other side of the coin, 36.36 percent of community colleges say they have not digitize much, while another 36.36 percent do not even have special collections in the first place. Those participants with an enrollment of at least 7,500 students are more active than those with smaller enrollments, as 42.86 percent of them report having digitized small-scale projects while another 28.57 percent report having made a significant effort to digitize (the only participants in the sample to do so). This trend is even more pronounced when the data is broken out by annual tuition: while just 20 percent of participants with an annual tuition under $5,000 say they have completed small-scale projects or else made significant efforts to digitize, this figure jumps to 57.14 percent for the middle tuition range ($5,000 to $14,999) and then up to 85.72 percent among those in the top tuition range ($15,000 or more).

The Future of Digitizing Special Collections

For 75 percent of the libraries in the sample, the digitization of special collections is "definitely in the plans, but [we] are just getting started." However, the remaining respondents say they "won't be doing much of this in the future." Much of these participants belonging to the latter group are institutions with 7,500 or more students, as 42.86 percent of them foresee the future of digitization of special collections in this way, compared to just 11.11 percent of those in the 2,500 to 7,499 enrollment range and 12.5 percent of those with enrollments under 2,500. Also of note is that while just 63.64 percent of community colleges and 71.43 percent of PhD-granting colleges and research universities have definitive plans that are just getting started, 100 percent of the four-year BA- or MA-granting colleges in the sample are at this point.

CHAPTER 11 – SPENDING TRENDS

Spending Plans in the Next Year

We asked survey participants their spending plans over the next year concerning a host of library costs and expenditures. Their choices were as follows: decrease substantially; decrease; remain the same; increase; increase substantially; or no current or planned spending.

Spending on Video Streaming

41.67 percent of all survey participants say they have "no current or planned spending" for video streaming, while another 33.33 percent say their spending on video streaming will "remain the same." This leaves just 16.67 percent who believe it will "increase," 4.17 percent who say it will "increase substantially," and 4.17 percent who say it will "decrease." Broken out by type of college, an overwhelming 85.71 percent of PhD-granting colleges and research universities in the sample do no have a current spending plan for this, while 45.45 percent of community colleges and 50 percent of four-year BA- and MA-granting colleges say this spending will remain the same. There is not much of a variation when broken out by enrollment, with most breakouts here falling between 5 and 10 percentage points within the sample average. However, when broken out by annual tuition, 57.14 percent of those participants with an annual tuition of at least $5,000 have no current spending plans on this, compared to just 20 percent of all other participants who can say the same.

Spending on Digital Repository Software and Services

While 41.67 percent of all survey participants do not have any current or planned spending for digital repository software and services in the next year, 20.83 percent expect their spending efforts to remain the same and another 20.83 percent believe spending will increase. PhD-granting colleges and research universities are particularly optimistic in this regard, as 42.86 percent of them believe spending will increase (and another 14.29 percent believe it will increase substantially, the only type of college to believe this to be the case). No more than 16.67 percent of any other type of college in the sample expects spending to increase here. 75 percent of the smallest colleges by enrollment (less than 2,500) do not have any current or planned spending for digital repository software and services, a figure which is no higher than 28.57 percent for all other enrollment ranges. In fact, 42.86 percent of participants with 7,500 or more students believe spending on this will increase in the next year.

Spending on Cloud Computing Web Storage Services

Over half (54.17 percent) of all survey participants do not have any current spending plans for cloud computing web storage services. However, just one participant believes it will decrease by any degree, while 25 percent believe it will increase, including 42.86 percent of PhD-granting colleges and research universities. The larger schools by enrollment are more likely to experience an increase in spending here, as 42.86 percent of those in the top enrollment bracket (7,500 or more) do, compared to just 12.5 percent of those in the lowest bracket (less than 2,500). Likewise, 57.14 percent of those schools with the highest tuitions ($15,000 or more) also anticipate spending on cloud computing to increase, while no more than 14.29 percent of all other participants expect the same.

Spending on RFID, Barcoding, and Other Inventory-Tracking Technologies

Just a shade less than half (45.83 percent) of all survey participants do not have any current spending plans over the next year for RFID, barcoding, and other inventory-tracking technologies. Many of these are participants with higher enrollments, as 57.14 percent of those participants in the top enrollment bracket do not have a plan, compared to just 37.5 percent of those in the lowest enrollment bracket. Nearly three-quarters (71.43 percent) of those participants in the middle tuition range ($5,000 to $14,999) think spending here will remain the same, yet no participants in the highest tuition range ($15,000 or more) can say the same. What's more, 28.57 percent of participants in the latter group think spending will decrease, the only survey participants to believe this to be the case.

Spending on Book- or Serials-Binding Technology and Services

Half of all survey participants believe spending next year on book- or serials-binding technology and services will decrease in some regard, and half of those believe it will decrease "substantially." No survey participants believe spending will increase by any measure, while 29.17 percent expect it to remain the same. Whereas 57.14 percent of participants in the top enrollment bracket and 66.67 percent of those in the middle bracket believe spending will decrease in some way, this is true for just 25 percent of those in the lowest enrollment bracket. A full two-thirds of four-year BA- or MA-granting colleges in the sample say spending will "decrease substantially," a figure which is no higher than 18.18 percent for all other participants.

Spending on Artwork for the Library

41.67 percent of all survey participants do not have any current spending plans regarding artwork for the library. While 20.83 percent believe it will "increase," another 20.83 percent say it will "remain the same." The only participants expecting a decrease here are those institutions with less than 7,500 students. On the other hand, 42.86 percent of survey participants with an enrollment of at least 7,500 think spending on library artwork will "increase," compared to only 12.5 percent of those in the bottom enrollment range and 11.11 percent of those in the middle range.

Spending on Whiteboards and Other Presentation/Testing Technologies

Nearly half (45.83 percent) of all participants do not have a current spending plan when it comes to whiteboards, classroom clickers, and other presentation/testing technologies. 29.17 percent think it will "remain the same," while the remaining 25 percent are evenly split between expecting an increase of any kind and expecting a decrease. The four-year BA- or MA-granting colleges in the sample are the only type of college not anticipating a decrease in spending, What's more, 50 percent of these participants think spending will remain the same. The smaller the institution by enrollment, the more likely it is the library does not have a spending plan for whiteboards and other presentation/testing technologies for the next year: while 28.57 percent of participants in the top enrollment range do not have such a plan, this figure increases to 44.44 percent for the middle enrollment bracket and then jumps again to 62.5 percent for the bottom bracket.

Spending on Mobile Computing and Telecommunications Devices

While 37.5 percent of libraries in the sample do not have a current spending plan for mobile computing and telecommunications devices over the next year, an identical 37.5 percent say spending will "increase" over this time. Just one participant believes spending will decrease by any measure here, as well as just one participant believes spending will "increase substantially." Nearly three-quarters (71.43 percent) of survey participants with an enrollment of at least 7,500 say spending will "increase" in the next year, by far the highest percentage among all libraries in this category: just 11.11 percent of participants in the middle enrollment range (2,500 to 7,499) say the same.

Spending on Library Public Relations and Marketing Services

A third of all libraries in the sample estimate that spending on public relations and marketing services for the library will remain the same over the next year. Another 29.17 percent believe it will increase over this time, while a quarter of all participants do not have a spending plan at all for such services. Community colleges are expected to be the steadiest here, as 45.45 percent of them say spending will remain the same and no community colleges expect a decrease of any size, the only type of college in the sample to do so. As enrollment increases, so too does the likelihood of spending on public relations increases: just 12.5 percent of participants in the bottom enrollment range (less than 2,500) say spending will "increase," a figure which nearly triples to 33.33 percent for the middle range (2,500 to 7,499) before increasing again to 42.86 percent for the top range (7,500 or more).

Spending on Applications Software

Regarding spending plans for applications software for media and computer centers/information commons, the majority of survey participants (83.34 percent) are evenly split between not having any current plans and expecting what spending plans they do have to remain the same. Just one participant each believes spending will "decrease" or "increase substantially," while the remaining two participants believe it will simply "increase." While 60 percent of those participants with an annual tuition less than $5,000 believe spending will remain the same here, the same can be said for just 28.57 percent of all other participants.

Spending on Librarian Travel and Conferences

Two-thirds of all survey participants say spending on librarian travel and conferences will remain the same for next year. Of the eight remaining participants, two believe it will "decrease substantially" while three believe it will simply "decrease" (and four of these five participants are community colleges). Two libraries believe spending on librarian travel and conferences will "increase," while the last remaining participant has no current spending plans for this. PhD-granting colleges and research universities are particularly steadfast in believing spending will remain the same, with 85.71 percent of them believing this to be the case (compared to just 54.55 percent for the community colleges..

Spending on Librarian Staff Training

70.83 percent of participants say spending on librarian staff training will remain the same, including 85.71 percent of participants with at least 7,500 students and 85.71 percent of PhD-granting colleges and research universities in the sample. Only three participants from the entire sample expect any sort of decrease, while another three participants expect an increase. The largest participants by total full-time enrollment are the mostly expecting no change in spending, with 85.71 percent of those libraries in the top enrollment bracket (7,500 or more) rating their future on staff training spending this way, while 25 percent of all those participants with enrollments under 2,500 expect spending to decrease in some way.

CHAPTER 12 – COMPUTING DEVICES AND LIBRARY INFORMATION TECHNOLOGY

Lending Laptops

Nearly half (45.83 percent) of all survey participants lend laptop computers to library patrons. The biggest proponents of this are the four-year BA-/MA-granting colleges, with 66.67 percent of them maintaining this practice, compared to just 42.86 percent of PhD-granting colleges and research universities and 36.36 percent of community colleges in the sample. Interestingly, between 57 and 62.5 percent of both the smallest and largest institutions by enrollment lend laptops, while only 22.22 percent of those participants in the middle enrollment range (2,500 to 7,499) do the same. Public schools (47.37 percent) maintain a slight edge over the private schools in the sample (40 percent).

Lending Tablet Computers

Just 16.67 percent of all libraries in the sample lend tablet computers to patrons, all of which are public schools with enrollments of at least 2,500 and annual tuitions under $15,000. Broken out by type of college, 33.33 percent of four-year BA-/MA-granting colleges in the sample lend tablet computers to patrons, while the same can be said for just 9.09 percent of community colleges and 14.29 percent of PhD-granting colleges and research universities.

Lending E-Book Reading Devices

29.17 percent of survey participants lend e-book reading devices to library patrons. There is not much variation when the data is broken out by type of college, as all three categories range between 27.27 and 33.33 percent here—likewise when the data is broken out by enrollment (between 25 and 33.33 percent). The biggest discrepancy arises when the data is broken out by annual tuition: while 20 percent of those libraries in the bottom tuition bracket (less than $5,000) and 28.57 percent of those in the top tuition bracket ($15,000 or more) lend e-book reading devices to library patrons, this figure jumps to 42.86 percent for the middle tuition range ($5,000 to $14,999).

Stock of Laptops

Among those participants that lend laptop computers to library patrons, the mean total stock of such devices available for loan is 27.36. The median is 20, and the range is from 2 to 100. The four-year BA-/MA-granting colleges have the most laptops here with a mean of 41.5, nearly twice that of the next closest mean of 22.67 belonging to the PhD-granting colleges and research universities. When broken out by enrollment, it's clear the larger institutions have more laptops at their disposal: those libraries in the middle (2,500 to 7,499) and top (7,500 or more) enrollment brackets have a mean of 42.5 and 42.75 laptops available to lend, respectively, while those in the bottom enrollment bracket (less than 2,500) have a mean of just 9.

Stock of Tablet Computers

The libraries in the sample that lend tablet computers to patrons have a mean of 14.25 such devices available for loan. However, this is a limited sample size, consisting of just four survey participants with the following number of tablets: 1; 6; 10; and 40. The participant with 40 tablets is a PhD-granting college or research university in both the middle tuition ($5,000 to $14,999) and enrollment (2,500 to 7,499) ranges.

Stock of E-Book Readers

The libraries in the sample that lend e-book reading devices to patrons have a mean of 7.71 such devices in stock. There are just seven participants that have such devices, with their respective totals as follows: 1; 2; 3; 3; 5; 10; and 30. No participant in either the top tuition bracket ($15,000 or more) or the bottom tuition bracket (less than $5,000) has more than 3 such devices available for loan.

Planned Spending on Laptop Computers

While our survey participants expect to spend a mean of $138.89 next year on laptop computers, this mean is the work of just one participant who plans to spend $2,500. No other libraries in the sample plan to spend any money on laptops within the next year. This lone participant is a community college with an enrollment between 2,500 and 7,499 and an annual tuition under $5,000.

Planned Spending on Tablet Computers and E-Book Reading Devices

Similarly, just three participants expect to spend anything on tablet computers within the next year, spending $1,000, $4,000, and $5,000, respectively. These three participants cover all three ranges of both annual tuition and full-time enrollment, two of which are four-year BA-/MA-granting colleges, the third of which is a community college.

No libraries in the sample expect to spend any money in the next year on e-book reading devices.

Chapter 1 – Staff

Table 1 What is the total staff of the library in terms of the number of full-time equivalent[1] positions?

Table 1.1.1 What is the total staff of the library in terms of the number of full-time equivalent positions?

	Mean	Median	Minimum	Maximum
Entire sample	16.38	10.00	1.80	80.00

Table 1.1.2 What is the total staff of the library in terms of the number of full-time equivalent positions? Broken out by type of college.

Type of College	Mean	Median	Minimum	Maximum
Community college	8.79	5.43	1.80	27.00
4-year BA- or MA-granting college	16.32	11.95	5.00	33.00
PhD-granting college or research university	28.36	12.00	8.00	80.00

Table 1.1.3 What is the total staff of the library in terms of the number of full-time equivalent positions? Broken out by full-time equivalent enrollment of the college.

Enrollment	Mean	Median	Minimum	Maximum
Less than 2,500	5.71	4.50	1.80	12.89
2,500 to 7,499	11.94	11.00	5.00	28.00
7,500 or more	34.29	28.00	10.00	80.00

[1] Includes full-time equivalent of all personnel (technical, clerical, professional, etc.)

Table 1.1.4 What is the total staff of the library in terms of the number of full-time equivalent positions? Broken out by public or private status of the college.

Public or Private	Mean	Median	Minimum	Maximum
Public	18.17	10.00	1.80	80.00
Private	9.58	10.00	5.00	12.89

Table 1.1.5 What is the total staff of the library in terms of the number of full-time equivalent positions? Broken out by annual full-time tuition prior to any deductions.

Tuition	Mean	Median	Minimum	Maximum
Less than $5,000	8.62	6.72	1.80	27.00
$5,000 to $14,999	25.57	14.50	2.00	80.00
$15,000 or more	18.27	12.00	5.00	52.00

Table 2 What is the total annual cost of salaries, benefits, and other compensation for the library in the 2013-14 academic year?

Table 2.1.1 What is the total annual cost of salaries, benefits, and other compensation for the library in the 2013-14 academic year?

	Mean	Median	Minimum	Maximum
Entire sample	$662,330.03	$361,000.00	$99,000.00	$3,304,860.00

Table 2.1.2 What is the total annual cost of salaries, benefits, and other compensation for the library in the 2013-14 academic year? Broken out by type of college.

Type of College	Mean	Median	Minimum	Maximum
Community college	$314,641.96	$210,900.00	$99,000.00	$648,000.00
4-year BA- or MA-granting college	$818,001.17	$559,745.00	$163,000.00	$2,025,517.00
PhD-granting college or research university	$1,101,363.20	$455,000.00	$170,000.00	$3,304,860.00

Table 2.1.3 What is the total annual cost of salaries, benefits, and other compensation for the library in the 2013-14 academic year? Broken out by full-time equivalent enrollment of the college.

Enrollment	Mean	Median	Minimum	Maximum
Less than 2,500	$203,982.13	$174,678.50	$99,000.00	$497,490.00
2,500 to 7,499	$529,545.83	$487,035.00	$170,000.00	$1,400,000.00
7,500 or more	$1,844,594.25	$1,712,758.50	$648,000.00	$3,304,860.00

Table 2.1.4 What is the total annual cost of salaries, benefits, and other compensation for the library in the 2013-14 academic year? Broken out by public or private status of the college.

Public or Private	Mean	Median	Minimum	Maximum
Public	$745,694.41	$393,035.00	$99,000.00	$3,304,860.00
Private	$328,872.50	$327,500.00	$163,000.00	$497,490.00

Table 2.1.5 What is the total annual cost of salaries, benefits, and other compensation for the library in the 2013-14 academic year? Broken out by annual full-time tuition prior to any deductions.

Tuition	Mean	Median	Minimum	Maximum
Less than $5,000	$290,157.13	$193,928.00	$99,000.00	$648,000.00
$5,000 to $14,999	$817,498.93	$555,733.30	$170,000.00	$2,025,517.00
$15,000 or more	$1,003,391.67	$476,245.00	$163,000.00	$3,304,860.00

Table 3 Over the past year, how have the salaries and benefits for the librarians employed by your institution changed?

Table 3.1.1 Over the past year, how have the salaries and benefits for the librarians employed by your institution changed?

	More or less declined	Kept up with inflation	Increased by less than 5%	Increased by more than 5%
Entire sample	70.83%	16.67%	12.50%	0.00%

Table 3.1.2 Over the past year, how have the salaries and benefits for the librarians employed by your institution changed? Broken out by type of college.

Type of College	More or less declined	Kept up with inflation	Increased by less than 5%	Increased by more than 5%
Community college	81.82%	18.18%	0.00%	0.00%
4-year BA- or MA-granting college	50.00%	0.00%	50.00%	0.00%
PhD-granting college or research university	71.43%	28.57%	0.00%	0.00%

Table 3.1.3 Over the past year, how have the salaries and benefits for the librarians employed by your institution changed? Broken out by full-time equivalent enrollment of the college.

Enrollment	More or less declined	Kept up with inflation	Increased by less than 5%	Increased by more than 5%
Less than 2,500	50.00%	25.00%	25.00%	0.00%
2,500 to 7,499	100.00%	0.00%	0.00%	0.00%
7,500 or more	57.14%	28.57%	14.29%	0.00%

Table 3.1.4 Over the past year, how have the salaries and benefits for the librarians employed by your institution changed? Broken out by public or private status of the college.

Public or Private	More or less declined	Kept up with inflation	Increased by less than 5%	Increased by more than 5%
Public	78.95%	15.79%	5.26%	0.00%
Private	40.00%	20.00%	40.00%	0.00%

Table 3.1.5 Over the past year, how have the salaries and benefits for the librarians employed by your institution changed? Broken out by annual full-time tuition prior to any deductions.

Tuition	More or less declined	Kept up with inflation	Increased by less than 5%	Increased by more than 5%
Less than $5,000	80.00%	20.00%	0.00%	0.00%
$5,000 to $14,999	85.71%	0.00%	14.29%	0.00%
$15,000 or more	42.86%	28.57%	28.57%	0.00%

Table 4 What was the total percentage change, if any, in the number of librarians[1] employed by your institution for the 2013-14 academic year?

Table 4.1.1 What was the total percentage change, if any, in the number of librarians employed by your institution for the 2013-14 academic year?

	Mean	Median	Minimum	Maximum
Entire sample	-2.88%	0.00%	-25.00%	2.00%

Table 4.1.2 What was the total percentage change, if any, in the number of librarians employed by your institution for the 2013-14 academic year? Broken out by type of college.

Type of College	Mean	Median	Minimum	Maximum
Community college	-2.45%	0.00%	-25.00%	0.00%
4-year BA- or MA-granting college	-2.33%	0.00%	-15.00%	1.00%
PhD-granting college or research university	-4.00%	0.00%	-20.00%	2.00%

Table 4.1.3 What was the total percentage change, if any, in the number of librarians employed by your institution for the 2013-14 academic year? Broken out by full-time equivalent enrollment of the college.

Enrollment	Mean	Median	Minimum	Maximum
Less than 2,500	-3.00%	0.00%	-25.00%	1.00%
2,500 to 7,499	-1.89%	0.00%	-15.00%	0.00%
7,500 or more	-4.00%	0.00%	-20.00%	2.00%

[1] Not support staff

Table 4.1.4 What was the total percentage change, if any, in the number of librarians employed by your institution for the 2013-14 academic year? Broken out by public or private status of the college.

Public or Private	Mean	Median	Minimum	Maximum
Public	-2.63%	0.00%	-25.00%	2.00%
Private	-3.80%	0.00%	-20.00%	1.00%

Table 4.1.5 What was the total percentage change, if any, in the number of librarians employed by your institution for the 2013-14 academic year? Broken out by annual full-time tuition prior to any deductions.

Tuition	Mean	Median	Minimum	Maximum
Less than $5,000	-2.70%	0.00%	-25.00%	0.00%
$5,000 to $14,999	-1.86%	0.00%	-15.00%	2.00%
$15,000 or more	-4.14%	0.00%	-20.00%	1.00%

Chapter 2 – Student Workers

Table 5 How many students work in your library?

Table 5.1.1 How many students work in your library?

	Mean	Median	Minimum	Maximum
Entire sample	11.20	7.00	0.00	80.00

Table 5.1.2 How many students work in your library? Broken out by type of college.

Type of College	Mean	Median	Minimum	Maximum
Community college	3.50	2.00	0.00	8.00
4-year BA- or MA-granting college	24.08	13.25	8.00	80.00
PhD-granting college or research university	11.14	10.00	0.00	24.00

Table 5.1.3 How many students work in your library? Broken out by full-time equivalent enrollment of the college.

Enrollment	Mean	Median	Minimum	Maximum
Less than 2,500	4.94	2.00	0.00	16.50
2,500 to 7,499	7.67	7.00	2.00	20.00
7,500 or more	24.83	17.00	4.00	80.00

Table 5.1.4 How many students work in your library? Broken out by public or private status of the college.

Public or Private	Mean	Median	Minimum	Maximum
Public	11.28	5.50	0.00	80.00
Private	10.90	10.00	6.00	16.50

Table 5.1.5 How many students work in your library? Broken out by annual full-time tuition prior to any deductions.

Tuition	Mean	Median	Minimum	Maximum
Less than $5,000	3.22	2.00	0.00	10.00
$5,000 to $14,999	20.86	10.00	1.00	80.00
$15,000 or more	11.79	10.00	4.00	24.00

Table 6 What is the average number of hours worked per week for the students who work in your library?

Table 6.1.1 What is the average number of hours worked per week for the students who work in your library?

	Mean	Median	Minimum	Maximum
Entire sample	11.25	12.00	5.00	20.00

Table 6.1.2 What is the average number of hours worked per week for the students who work in your library? Broken out by type of college.

Type of College	Mean	Median	Minimum	Maximum
Community college	14.28	15.00	7.00	20.00
4-year BA- or MA-granting college	12.58	13.50	5.00	20.00
PhD-granting college or research university	10.33	10.00	5.00	15.00

Table 6.1.3 What is the average number of hours worked per week for the students who work in your library? Broken out by full-time equivalent enrollment of the college.

Enrollment	Mean	Median	Minimum	Maximum
Less than 2,500	9.92	8.75	5.00	15.00
2,500 to 7,499	14.94	15.00	5.00	20.00
7,500 or more	12.00	11.00	10.00	18.00

Table 6.1.4 What is the average number of hours worked per week for the students who work in your library? Broken out by public or private status of the college.

Public or Private	Mean	Median	Minimum	Maximum
Public	13.22	13.00	5.00	20.00
Private	10.90	12.00	5.00	15.00

Table 6.1.5 What is the average number of hours worked per week for the students who work in your library? Broken out by annual full-time tuition prior to any deductions.

Tuition	Mean	Median	Minimum	Maximum
Less than $5,000	14.64	15.00	10.00	18.00
$5,000 to $14,999	12.71	12.00	5.00	20.00
$15,000 or more	10.64	10.00	5.00	15.00

Table 7 What is the average hourly rate of pay (in USD) for the students who work in the library?

Table 7.1.1 What is the average hourly rate of pay (in USD) for the students who work in the library?

	Mean	Median	Minimum	Maximum
Entire sample	$8.71	$7.85	$5.15	$21.34

Table 7.1.2 What is the average hourly rate of pay (in USD) for the students who work in the library? Broken out by type of college.

Type of College	Mean	Median	Minimum	Maximum
Community college	$7.92	$7.50	$7.25	$10.90
4-year BA- or MA-granting college	$7.39	$7.48	$5.15	$9.00
PhD-granting college or research university	$11.71	$8.50	$8.00	$21.34

Table 7.1.3 What is the average hourly rate of pay (in USD) for the students who work in the library? Broken out by full-time equivalent enrollment of the college.

Enrollment	Mean	Median	Minimum	Maximum
Less than 2,500	$8.15	$7.75	$7.25	$10.90
2,500 to 7,499	$7.88	$7.50	$5.15	$12.70
7,500 or more	$10.87	$8.00	$8.00	$21.34

Table 7.1.4 What is the average hourly rate of pay (in USD) for the students who work in the library? Broken out by public or private status of the college.

Public or Private	Mean	Median	Minimum	Maximum
Public	$8.95	$7.85	$5.15	$21.34
Private	$7.75	$7.63	$7.25	$8.50

Table 7.1.5 What is the average hourly rate of pay (in USD) for the students who work in the library? Broken out by annual full-time tuition prior to any deductions.

Tuition	Mean	Median	Minimum	Maximum
Less than $5,000	$7.69	$7.50	$5.15	$10.90
$5,000 to $14,999	$8.58	$8.00	$7.25	$12.70
$15,000 or more	$10.06	$8.00	$7.25	$21.34

Describe the library training, if any, your student workers receive.

1. Total immersion during the first two weeks of employment: circulation, shelving, Dewey Decimal, customer service, filing, plant watering, serials ad inf.

2. FERPA tutorial, LC Easy tutorial, training workbook, orientation meeting, 1:1 instruction.

3. Full training in circulation functions and basic training for answering enquiries. We operate a triage system, so, those on the frontline answer basic questions and refer any questions that require detailed knowledge of collections/ e-resources.

4. Usually hired singly, and trained one on one.

5. On the job.

6. Orientation and technology.

7. All students go through training in service excellence and in department that hires them fro specific areas of responsibility.

8. Training on LC and training for how to shelve, check out a resource, put an item on hold, make photocopies, and file back periodicals.

9. OJT.

10. On the job training.

11. Taught to work the library ILS - specifically circulation, how to shelve using LC, answer the telephone in a professional manner, fix simple equipment issues.

12. 10 hours watching then doing circulation, shelving, cleaning, watering, delivering equipment.

13. Customer service, checking opac, ILL, archival standards; it depends on where they work.

14. Learning LC call number sequence. Data management.

15. They work one-on-one with a staff member, following a training plan for two weeks. They then work at the desk by themselves with assistance from

Library staff.

16. Manual handling, introduction to Dewey, introduction to admin tasks.

17. Orientation to library procedures and policies, job specific training based on area they work in.

18. Individual orientation/training session by circ coordinator.

19. Librarians go over work assignments.

20. Training initially when they start working and then monthly updates.

Chapter 3 – Changes in the Deployment of Labor

Describe any significant changes in the way the library has deployed labor in the past few years (or any upcoming plans for changes). Have you increase (or plan to increase) the number of full- or part-time positions in a given division? Have you been able to increase productivity in a division and make do with less labor?

1. Empty technical services positions will be filled with positions in other areas of library.

2. Moved a part-time librarian to full-time, absorbing a full-time Circulation position vacant due to retirement.

3. We have redefined our student employee positions in order to meet changing needs.

4. Have been attempting to get an additional position for 4 years, no luck yet.

5. As minimum wage has gone up, I lose more hours of student help. There is no hope of additional staff. Admin would close physical library if they could.

6. Increasing adjunct librarian duties and cross-training workers in public and technical services helps with project work and times of heavy work loads.

7. We've lost 3 of 6 librarians in the last 5 years, including one at the end of this academic year.

8. No, No.

9. All staffing including students has been reduced by 387.3% per student enrolled over a 10 year period. Pay adjusted for inflation has been reduced by about 30% over that same time. To be fair usage has decreased dramatically as well. We are currently beginning to look at disestablishing the traditional library and its services.

10. In the past few years the professional and para-professional staffing of the library service has been reduced, with some of the capacity being taken up by student shelvers.

11. We have had to do more with less. To increase hours, we made our staffing more efficient by not requiring multiple staff at all times (we now will have 1 person on, but that is infrequent, but 2 is very common). This has allowed us to be open later during the week and to add a weekend day.

12. We've had a labor shortage for the past 7 years. Looks like that has become the new normal.

13. Organizational changes to maximize experience and expertise in certain areas.

14. We have been able to hire temporary help in the evenings where before each staff member had to work 1 night a week. This has enabled us to boost productivity during the day.

15. No increase in the number of staff.

16. Increased reference and instruction.

17. When we have a technical services retirement, the position will be restructured to provide more direct patron services to cover all library hours. Already slightly understaffed for general services, so we cannot reduce staffing further.

18. We have consolidated from 5 into 3 Libraries which has also brought about a reduction in staffing. We deploy fewer staff at frontline information desks and have created a Learning Technologist post. Productivity has increased in terms of fewer information points which therefore have more students accessing them. The move from print books to e-books has also meant a small reduction in shelving and we have reduced staff accordingly.

19. Neither.

20. We have run lean for quite a while. We are giving more of our basic duties to our part-time night and weekend librarians and staff members.

21. Added another library administrator. Technical services is working with 2 less full-time positions that have not and will not be filled. Even though circulation has plummeted, we have the exact same number of circulation aides at the circ desk.

22. Nothing.

23. We have lost one full-time and one part-time position which the college refuses to fill. Productivity has been compromised.

Table 8 As a general rule, how do you expect resource allocation to the library over the next few years to stack up vis-à-vis other academic departments in your institution?

Table 8.1.1 As a general rule, how do you expect resource allocation to the library over the next few years to stack up vis-à-vis other academic departments in your institution?

	We expect to do better than other departments	We expect to keep pace with other departments	We expect to do worse than other departments
Entire sample	4.17%	50.00%	45.83%

Table 8.1.2 As a general rule, how do you expect resource allocation to the library over the next few years to stack up vis-à-vis other academic departments in your institution? Broken out by type of college.

Type of College	We expect to do better than other departments	We expect to keep pace with other departments	We expect to do worse than other departments
Community college	9.09%	36.36%	54.55%
4-year BA- or MA-granting college	0.00%	66.67%	33.33%
PhD-granting college or research university	0.00%	57.14%	42.86%

Table 8.1.3 As a general rule, how do you expect resource allocation to the library over the next few years to stack up vis-à-vis other academic departments in your institution? Broken out by full-time equivalent enrollment of the college.

Enrollment	We expect to do better than other departments	We expect to keep pace with other departments	We expect to do worse than other departments
Less than 2,500	12.50%	37.50%	50.00%
2,500 to 7,499	0.00%	88.89%	11.11%
7,500 or more	0.00%	14.29%	85.71%

Table 8.1.4 As a general rule, how do you expect resource allocation to the library over the next few years to stack up vis-à-vis other academic departments in your institution? Broken out by public or private status of the college.

Public or Private	We expect to do better than other departments	We expect to keep pace with other departments	We expect to do worse than other departments
Public	5.26%	47.37%	47.37%
Private	0.00%	60.00%	40.00%

Table 8.1.5 As a general rule, how do you expect resource allocation to the library over the next few years to stack up vis-à-vis other academic departments in your institution? Broken out by annual full-time tuition prior to any deductions.

Tuition	We expect to do better than other departments	We expect to keep pace with other departments	We expect to do worse than other departments
Less than $5,000	10.00%	40.00%	50.00%
$5,000 to $14,999	0.00%	57.14%	42.86%
$15,000 or more	0.00%	57.14%	42.86%

The Survey of Academic Libraries, 2014-15 Edition

Chapter 4 – Materials & A/V Spending

Table 9 What is the library's total spending on materials/content[1] for the 2013-14 academic year?

Table 9.1.1 What is the library's total spending on materials/content for the 2013-14 academic year?

	Mean	Median	Minimum	Maximum
Entire sample	$628,273.52	$120,000.00	$20,425.00	$5,000,000.00

Table 9.1.2 What is the library's total spending on materials/content for the 2013-14 academic year? Broken out by type of college.

Type of College	Mean	Median	Minimum	Maximum
Community college	$116,110.90	$58,029.50	$31,765.00	$591,085.00
4-year BA- or MA-granting college	$432,642.00	$400,000.00	$75,000.00	$825,792.00
PhD-granting college or research university	$1,644,904.17	$967,500.00	$20,425.00	$5,000,000.00

---

[1] Includes books, e-books, online databases, CD-ROM/DVD/tape databases, audio-visual resources, journals, magazines, directories, and other periodicals

Table 9.1.3 What is the library's total spending on materials/content for the 2013-14 academic year? Broken out by full-time equivalent enrollment of the college.

Enrollment	Mean	Median	Minimum	Maximum
Less than 2,500	$141,604.00	$53,012.00	$20,425.00	$732,418.00
2,500 to 7,499	$226,290.71	$101,000.00	$50,000.00	$500,000.00
7,500 or more	$1,746,146.17	$1,130,396.00	$120,000.00	$5,000,000.00

Table 9.1.4 What is the library's total spending on materials/content for the 2013-14 academic year? Broken out by public or private status of the college.

Public or Private	Mean	Median	Minimum	Maximum
Public	$691,548.59	$101,000.00	$20,425.00	$5,000,000.00
Private	$359,354.50	$315,000.00	$75,000.00	$732,418.00

Table 9.1.5 What is the library's total spending on materials/content for the 2013-14 academic year? Broken out by annual full-time tuition prior to any deductions.

Tuition	Mean	Median	Minimum	Maximum
Less than $5,000	$154,814.89	$60,035.00	$20,425.00	$591,085.00
$5,000 to $14,999	$1,070,498.67	$255,000.00	$37,200.00	$5,000,000.00
$15,000 or more	$896,236.33	$616,209.00	$75,000.00	$2,505,000.00

Table 10 By how much did materials spending change (not accounting for inflation) in the 2013-14 academic year?

Table 10.1.1 By how much did materials spending change (not accounting for inflation) in the 2013-14 academic year?

	Mean	Median	Minimum	Maximum
Entire sample	0.38%	0.00%	-30.00%	30.00%

Table 10.1.2 By how much did materials spending change (not accounting for inflation) in the 2013-14 academic year? Broken out by type of college.

Type of College	Mean	Median	Minimum	Maximum
Community college	1.55%	0.00%	-30.00%	30.00%
4-year BA- or MA-granting college	-1.75%	0.00%	-7.00%	0.00%
PhD-granting college or research university	-0.33%	0.00%	-5.00%	3.00%

Table 10.1.3 By how much did materials spending change (not accounting for inflation) in the 2013-14 academic year? Broken out by full-time equivalent enrollment of the college.

Enrollment	Mean	Median	Minimum	Maximum
Less than 2,500	-5.00%	0.00%	-30.00%	5.00%
2,500 to 7,499	3.13%	0.00%	-8.00%	30.00%
7,500 or more	3.00%	0.00%	-7.00%	30.00%

Table 10.1.4 By how much did materials spending change (not accounting for inflation) in the 2013-14 academic year? Broken out by public or private status of the college.

Public or Private	Mean	Median	Minimum	Maximum
Public	0.59%	0.00%	-30.00%	30.00%
Private	-0.50%	0.00%	-5.00%	3.00%

Table 10.1.5 By how much did materials spending change (not accounting for inflation) in the 2013-14 academic year? Broken out by annual full-time tuition prior to any deductions.

Tuition	Mean	Median	Minimum	Maximum
Less than $5,000	1.70%	0.00%	-10.00%	30.00%
$5,000 to $14,999	-1.17%	0.00%	-30.00%	30.00%
$15,000 or more	-0.40%	0.00%	-5.00%	3.00%

Table 11 By how much do you expect materials spending to change in the 2014-15 academic year?

Table 11.1.1 By how much do you expect materials spending to change in the 2014-15 academic year?

	Mean	Median	Minimum	Maximum
Entire sample	0.23%	0.00%	-25.00%	25.00%

Table 11.1.2 By how much do you expect materials spending to change in the 2014-15 academic year? Broken out by type of college.

Type of College	Mean	Median	Minimum	Maximum
Community college	-0.09%	0.00%	-25.00%	25.00%
4-year BA- or MA-granting college	1.20%	0.00%	0.00%	6.00%
PhD-granting college or research university	0.00%	0.00%	-5.00%	3.00%

Table 11.1.3 By how much do you expect materials spending to change in the 2014-15 academic year? Broken out by full-time equivalent enrollment of the college.

Enrollment	Mean	Median	Minimum	Maximum
Less than 2,500	-2.50%	0.00%	-25.00%	5.00%
2,500 to 7,499	-0.38%	0.00%	-6.00%	3.00%
7,500 or more	4.67%	1.00%	-5.00%	25.00%

Table 11.1.4 By how much do you expect materials spending to change in the 2014-15 academic year? Broken out by public or private status of the college.

Public or Private	Mean	Median	Minimum	Maximum
Public	0.41%	0.00%	-25.00%	25.00%
Private	-0.40%	0.00%	-5.00%	3.00%

Table 11.1.5 By how much do you expect materials spending to change in the 2014-15 academic year? Broken out by annual full-time tuition prior to any deductions.

Tuition	Mean	Median	Minimum	Maximum
Less than $5,000	-0.10%	0.00%	-25.00%	25.00%
$5,000 to $14,999	1.33%	0.00%	0.00%	6.00%
$15,000 or more	-0.33%	0.00%	-5.00%	3.00%

Table 12 How much will the library spend for information accessed online in the 2013-14 academic year?

Table 12.1.1 How much will the library spend for information accessed online in the 2013-14 academic year?

	Mean	Median	Minimum	Maximum
Entire sample	$305,559.57	$60,000.00	$6,000.00	$2,152,000.00

Table 12.1.2 How much will the library spend for information accessed online in the 2013-14 academic year? Broken out by type of college.

Type of College	Mean	Median	Minimum	Maximum
Community college	$73,109.09	$33,000.00	$6,000.00	$346,200.00
4-year BA- or MA-granting college	$339,786.25	$304,572.50	$50,000.00	$700,000.00
PhD-granting college or research university	$708,901.00	$335,000.00	$13,617.00	$2,152,000.00

Table 12.1.3 How much will the library spend for information accessed online in the 2013-14 academic year? Broken out by full-time equivalent enrollment of the college.

Enrollment	Mean	Median	Minimum	Maximum
Less than 2,500	$92,720.25	$25,000.00	$6,000.00	$531,145.00
2,500 to 7,499	$127,541.29	$60,000.00	$27,000.00	$350,000.00
7,500 or more	$797,033.33	$523,100.00	$54,000.00	$2,152,000.00

Table 12.1.4 How much will the library spend for information accessed online in the 2013-14 academic year? Broken out by public or private status of the college.

Public or Private	Mean	Median	Minimum	Maximum
Public	$318,094.47	$54,000.00	$6,000.00	$2,152,000.00
Private	$252,286.25	$214,000.00	$50,000.00	$531,145.00

Table 12.1.5 How much will the library spend for information accessed online in the 2013-14 academic year? Broken out by annual full-time tuition prior to any deductions.

Tuition	Mean	Median	Minimum	Maximum
Less than $5,000	$79,757.44	$33,000.00	$6,000.00	$346,200.00
$5,000 to $14,999	$221,298.17	$133,894.50	$13,000.00	$700,000.00
$15,000 or more	$728,524.17	$440,572.50	$50,000.00	$2,152,000.00

Table 13 What was the rate of change in the library's spending on online content/information between the 2012-13 and 2013-14 academic years?

Table 13.1.1 What was the rate of change in the library's spending on online content/information between the 2012-13 and 2013-14 academic years?

	Mean	Median	Minimum	Maximum
Entire sample	3.95%	1.50%	-20.00%	24.00%

Table 13.1.2 What was the rate of change in the library's spending on online content/information between the 2012-13 and 2013-14 academic years? Broken out by type of college.

Type of College	Mean	Median	Minimum	Maximum
Community college	3.73%	5.00%	-20.00%	20.00%
4-year BA- or MA-granting college	5.80%	0.00%	0.00%	24.00%
PhD-granting college or research university	2.83%	1.50%	0.00%	7.00%

Table 13.1.3 What was the rate of change in the library's spending on online content/information between the 2012-13 and 2013-14 academic years? Broken out by full-time equivalent enrollment of the college.

Enrollment	Mean	Median	Minimum	Maximum
Less than 2,500	4.38%	2.50%	-20.00%	24.00%
2,500 to 7,499	2.13%	0.00%	0.00%	7.00%
7,500 or more	5.83%	4.00%	0.00%	20.00%

Table 13.1.4 What was the rate of change in the library's spending on online content/information between the 2012-13 and 2013-14 academic years? Broken out by public or private status of the college.

Public or Private	Mean	Median	Minimum	Maximum
Public	3.11%	1.50%	-20.00%	20.00%
Private	7.75%	3.50%	0.00%	24.00%

Table 13.1.5 What was the rate of change in the library's spending on online content/information between the 2012-13 and 2013-14 academic years? Broken out by annual full-time tuition prior to any deductions.

Tuition	Mean	Median	Minimum	Maximum
Less than $5,000	5.60%	2.50%	0.00%	20.00%
$5,000 to $14,999	-0.50%	2.50%	-20.00%	7.00%
$15,000 or more	5.67%	1.50%	0.00%	24.00%

Table 14 Over the past two years, how has the library's spending on video resources such as films, DVDs, film downloads via the web, and other video-streaming technologies changed?

Table 14.1.1 Over the past two years, how has the library's spending on video resources such as films, DVDs, film downloads via the web, and other video-streaming technologies changed?

	Declined	Remained the same	Increased by less than 5%	Increased by more than 5%
Entire sample	37.50%	37.50%	12.50%	12.50%

Table 14.1.2 Over the past two years, how has the library's spending on video resources such as films, DVDs, film downloads via the web, and other video-streaming technologies changed? Broken out by type of college.

Type of College	Declined	Remained the same	Increased by less than 5%	Increased by more than 5%
Community college	27.27%	36.36%	18.18%	18.18%
4-year BA- or MA-granting college	33.33%	33.33%	16.67%	16.67%
PhD-granting college or research university	57.14%	42.86%	0.00%	0.00%

Table 14.1.3 Over the past two years, how has the library's spending on video resources such as films, DVDs, film downloads via the web, and other video-streaming technologies changed? Broken out by full-time equivalent enrollment of the college.

Enrollment	Declined	Remained the same	Increased by less than 5%	Increased by more than 5%
Less than 2,500	37.50%	37.50%	25.00%	0.00%
2,500 to 7,499	33.33%	44.44%	11.11%	11.11%
7,500 or more	42.86%	28.57%	0.00%	28.57%

Table 14.1.4 Over the past two years, how has the library's spending on video resources such as films, DVDs, film downloads via the web, and other video-streaming technologies changed? Broken out by public or private status of the college.

Public or Private	Declined	Remained the same	Increased by less than 5%	Increased by more than 5%
Public	36.84%	36.84%	10.53%	15.79%
Private	40.00%	40.00%	20.00%	0.00%

Table 14.1.5 Over the past two years, how has the library's spending on video resources such as films, DVDs, film downloads via the web, and other video-streaming technologies changed? Broken out by annual full-time tuition prior to any deductions.

Tuition	Declined	Remained the same	Increased by less than 5%	Increased by more than 5%
Less than $5,000	30.00%	40.00%	20.00%	10.00%
$5,000 to $14,999	42.86%	28.57%	0.00%	28.57%
$15,000 or more	42.86%	42.86%	14.29%	0.00%

Table 15 What was the library's spending on audio-visual resources in the 2013-14 academic year?

Table 15.1.1 What was the library's spending on audio-visual resources in the 2013-14 academic year?

	Mean	Median	Minimum	Maximum
Entire sample	$9,231.33	$4,000.00	$0.00	$40,000.00

Table 15.1.2 What was the library's spending on audio-visual resources in the 2013-14 academic year? Broken out by type of college.

Type of College	Mean	Median	Minimum	Maximum
Community college	$8,411.00	$4,500.00	$0.00	$35,500.00
4-year BA- or MA-granting college	$10,063.50	$6,627.00	$2,000.00	$25,000.00
PhD-granting college or research university	$10,450.00	$900.00	$0.00	$40,000.00

Table 15.1.3 What was the library's spending on audio-visual resources in the 2013-14 academic year? Broken out by full-time equivalent enrollment of the college.

Enrollment	Mean	Median	Minimum	Maximum
Less than 2,500	$2,781.75	$1,400.00	$0.00	$8,254.00
2,500 to 7,499	$4,982.00	$3,000.00	$10.00	$15,000.00
7,500 or more	$23,800.00	$25,000.00	$1,500.00	$40,000.00

Table 15.1.4 What was the library's spending on audio-visual resources in the 2013-14 academic year? Broken out by public or private status of the college.

Public or Private	Mean	Median	Minimum	Maximum
Public	$10,757.86	$4,500.00	$0.00	$40,000.00
Private	$3,888.50	$3,500.00	$300.00	$8,254.00

Table 15.1.5 What was the library's spending on audio-visual resources in the 2013-14 academic year? Broken out by annual full-time tuition prior to any deductions.

Tuition	Mean	Median	Minimum	Maximum
Less than $5,000	$8,637.50	$4,500.00	$0.00	$35,500.00
$5,000 to $14,999	$16,002.00	$15,000.00	$0.00	$40,000.00
$15,000 or more	$3,410.80	$2,000.00	$300.00	$8,254.00

Table 16 What do you expect the library's spending on audio-visual resources to be in the 2014-15 academic year?

Table 16.1.1 What do you expect the library's spending on audio-visual resources to be in the 2014-15 academic year?

	Mean	Median	Minimum	Maximum
Entire sample	$8,789.44	$2,500.00	$0.00	$35,500.00

Table 16.1.2 What do you expect the library's spending on audio-visual resources to be in the 2014-15 academic year? Broken out by type of college.

Type of College	Mean	Median	Minimum	Maximum
Community college	$8,911.00	$4,000.00	$0.00	$35,500.00
4-year BA- or MA-granting college	$9,200.00	$4,900.00	$2,000.00	$25,000.00
PhD-granting college or research university	$8,075.00	$1,150.00	$0.00	$30,000.00

Table 16.1.3 What do you expect the library's spending on audio-visual resources to be in the 2014-15 academic year? Broken out by full-time equivalent enrollment of the college.

Enrollment	Mean	Median	Minimum	Maximum
Less than 2,500	$2,675.00	$1,250.00	$0.00	$9,000.00
2,500 to 7,499	$4,862.00	$3,000.00	$10.00	$16,000.00
7,500 or more	$22,500.00	$25,000.00	$2,000.00	$35,500.00

Table 16.1.4 What do you expect the library's spending on audio-visual resources to be in the 2014-15 academic year? Broken out by public or private status of the college.

Public or Private	Mean	Median	Minimum	Maximum
Public	$10,436.43	$4,000.00	$0.00	$35,500.00
Private	$3,025.00	$2,000.00	$300.00	$7,800.00

Table 16.1.5 What do you expect the library's spending on audio-visual resources to be in the 2014-15 academic year? Broken out by annual full-time tuition prior to any deductions.

Tuition	Mean	Median	Minimum	Maximum
Less than $5,000	$9,137.50	$4,000.00	$0.00	$35,500.00
$5,000 to $14,999	$14,202.00	$16,000.00	$0.00	$30,000.00
$15,000 or more	$2,820.00	$2,000.00	$300.00	$7,800.00

Chapter 5 – Grants

Table 17 Has the library received any grant support in the past year from any federal agencies?

Table 17.1.1 Has the library received any grant support in the past year from any federal agencies?

	No Answer	Yes	No
Entire sample	0.00%	8.33%	91.67%

Table 17.1.2 Has the library received any grant support in the past year from any federal agencies? Broken out by type of college.

Type of College	Yes	No
Community college	0.00%	100.00%
4-year BA- or MA-granting college	16.67%	83.33%
PhD-granting college or research university	14.29%	85.71%

Table 17.1.3 Has the library received any grant support in the past year from any federal agencies? Broken out by full-time equivalent enrollment of the college.

Enrollment	Yes	No
Less than 2,500	0.00%	100.00%
2,500 to 7,499	0.00%	100.00%
7,500 or more	28.57%	71.43%

Table 17.1.4 Has the library received any grant support in the past year from any federal agencies? Broken out by public or private status of the college.

Public or Private	Yes	No
Public	10.53%	89.47%
Private	0.00%	100.00%

Table 17.1.5 Has the library received any grant support in the past year from any federal agencies? Broken out by annual full-time tuition prior to any deductions.

Tuition	Yes	No
Less than $5,000	0.00%	100.00%
$5,000 to $14,999	28.57%	71.43%
$15,000 or more	0.00%	100.00%

Table 18 Has the library received any grant support in the past year from any state or local government agencies?

Table 18.1.1 Has the library received any grant support in the past year from any state or local government agencies?

	No Answer	Yes	No
Entire sample	0.00%	12.50%	87.50%

Table 18.1.2 Has the library received any grant support in the past year from any state or local government agencies? Broken out by type of college.

Type of College	Yes	No
Community college	0.00%	100.00%
4-year BA- or MA-granting college	16.67%	83.33%
PhD-granting college or research university	28.57%	71.43%

Table 18.1.3 Has the library received any grant support in the past year from any state or local government agencies? Broken out by full-time equivalent enrollment of the college.

Enrollment	Yes	No
Less than 2,500	25.00%	75.00%
2,500 to 7,499	0.00%	100.00%
7,500 or more	14.29%	85.71%

Table 18.1.4 Has the library received any grant support in the past year from any state or local government agencies? Broken out by public or private status of the college.

Public or Private	Yes	No
Public	10.53%	89.47%
Private	20.00%	80.00%

Table 18.1.5 Has the library received any grant support in the past year from any state or local government agencies? Broken out by annual full-time tuition prior to any deductions.

Tuition	Yes	No
Less than $5,000	10.00%	90.00%
$5,000 to $14,999	0.00%	100.00%
$15,000 or more	28.57%	71.43%

Table 19 Has the library received any grant support in the past year from any foundations?

Table 19.1.1 Has the library received any grant support in the past year from any foundations?

	No Answer	Yes	No
Entire sample	0.00%	8.33%	91.67%

Table 19.1.2 Has the library received any grant support in the past year from any foundations? Broken out by type of college.

Type of College	Yes	No
Community college	18.18%	81.82%
4-year BA- or MA-granting college	0.00%	100.00%
PhD-granting college or research university	0.00%	100.00%

Table 19.1.3 Has the library received any grant support in the past year from any foundations? Broken out by full-time equivalent enrollment of the college.

Enrollment	Yes	No
Less than 2,500	25.00%	75.00%
2,500 to 7,499	0.00%	100.00%
7,500 or more	0.00%	100.00%

Table 19.1.4 Has the library received any grant support in the past year from any foundations? Broken out by public or private status of the college.

Public or Private	Yes	No
Public	10.53%	89.47%
Private	0.00%	100.00%

Table 19.1.5 Has the library received any grant support in the past year from any foundations? Broken out by annual full-time tuition prior to any deductions.

Tuition	Yes	No
Less than $5,000	20.00%	80.00%
$5,000 to $14,999	0.00%	100.00%
$15,000 or more	0.00%	100.00%

Table 20 Has the library received any grant support in the past year from any private companies?

Table 20.1.1 Has the library received any grant support in the past year from any private companies?

	No Answer	Yes	No
Entire sample	0.00%	0.00%	100.00%

Table 21 Has the library received any grant support in the past year from any special funds of the university?

Table 21.1.1 Has the library received any grant support in the past year from any special funds of the university?

	No Answer	Yes	No
Entire sample	0.00%	4.17%	95.83%

Table 21.1.2 Has the library received any grant support in the past year from any special funds of the university? Broken out by type of college.

Type of College	Yes	No
Community college	9.09%	90.91%
4-year BA- or MA-granting college	0.00%	100.00%
PhD-granting college or research university	0.00%	100.00%

Table 21.1.3 Has the library received any grant support in the past year from any special funds of the university? Broken out by full-time equivalent enrollment of the college.

Enrollment	Yes	No
Less than 2,500	0.00%	100.00%
2,500 to 7,499	11.11%	88.89%
7,500 or more	0.00%	100.00%

Table 21.1.4 Has the library received any grant support in the past year from any special funds of the university? Broken out by public or private status of the college.

Public or Private	Yes	No
Public	5.26%	94.74%
Private	0.00%	100.00%

Table 21.1.5 Has the library received any grant support in the past year from any special funds of the university? Broken out by annual full-time tuition prior to any deductions.

Tuition	Yes	No
Less than $5,000	0.00%	100.00%
$5,000 to $14,999	14.29%	85.71%
$15,000 or more	0.00%	100.00%

Table 22 Has the library received any grant support in the past year from any alumni?

Table 22.1.1 Has the library received any grant support in the past year from any alumni?

	No Answer	Yes	No
Entire sample	0.00%	4.17%	95.83%

Table 22.1.2 Has the library received any grant support in the past year from any alumni? Broken out by type of college.

Type of College	Yes	No
Community college	0.00%	100.00%
4-year BA- or MA-granting college	0.00%	100.00%
PhD-granting college or research university	14.29%	85.71%

Table 22.1.3 Has the library received any grant support in the past year from any alumni? Broken out by full-time equivalent enrollment of the college.

Enrollment	Yes	No
Less than 2,500	0.00%	100.00%
2,500 to 7,499	0.00%	100.00%
7,500 or more	14.29%	85.71%

Table 22.1.4 Has the library received any grant support in the past year from any alumni? Broken out by public or private status of the college.

Public or Private	Yes	No
Public	5.26%	94.74%
Private	0.00%	100.00%

Table 22.1.5 Has the library received any grant support in the past year from any alumni? Broken out by annual full-time tuition prior to any deductions.

Tuition	Yes	No
Less than $5,000	0.00%	100.00%
$5,000 to $14,999	14.29%	85.71%
$15,000 or more	0.00%	100.00%

Table 23 What was the total value of spending derived from grants in the 2012-13 academic year?

Table 23.1.1 What was the total value of spending derived from grants in the 2012-13 academic year?

	Mean	Median	Minimum	Maximum
Entire sample	$1,385.00	$0.00	$0.00	$12,000.00

Table 23.1.2 What was the total value of spending derived from grants in the 2012-13 academic year? Broken out by type of college.

Type of College	Mean	Median	Minimum	Maximum
Community college	$927.27	$0.00	$0.00	$5,000.00
4-year BA- or MA-granting college	$4,250.00	$2,500.00	$0.00	$12,000.00
PhD-granting college or research university	$100.00	$0.00	$0.00	$500.00

Table 23.1.3 What was the total value of spending derived from grants in the 2012-13 academic year? Broken out by full-time equivalent enrollment of the college.

Enrollment	Mean	Median	Minimum	Maximum
Less than 2,500	$2,600.00	$0.00	$0.00	$12,000.00
2,500 to 7,499	$571.43	$0.00	$0.00	$4,000.00
7,500 or more	$916.67	$0.00	$0.00	$5,000.00

Table 23.1.4 What was the total value of spending derived from grants in the 2012-13 academic year? Broken out by public or private status of the college.

Public or Private	Mean	Median	Minimum	Maximum
Public	$923.53	$0.00	$0.00	$5,000.00
Private	$4,000.00	$0.00	$0.00	$12,000.00

Table 23.1.5 What was the total value of spending derived from grants in the 2012-13 academic year? Broken out by annual full-time tuition prior to any deductions.

Tuition	Mean	Median	Minimum	Maximum
Less than $5,000	$620.00	$0.00	$0.00	$5,000.00
$5,000 to $14,999	$1,800.00	$0.00	$0.00	$5,000.00
$15,000 or more	$2,500.00	$0.00	$0.00	$12,000.00

Table 24 What do you expect will be the total value of spending derived from grants in the 2013-14 academic year?

Table 24.1.1 What do you expect will be the total value of spending derived from grants in the 2013-14 academic year?

	Mean	Median	Minimum	Maximum
Entire sample	$665.00	$0.00	$0.00	$5,000.00

Table 24.1.2 What do you expect will be the total value of spending derived from grants in the 2013-14 academic year? Broken out by type of college.

Type of College	Mean	Median	Minimum	Maximum
Community college	$709.09	$0.00	$0.00	$4,000.00
4-year BA- or MA-granting college	$1,250.00	$0.00	$0.00	$5,000.00
PhD-granting college or research university	$100.00	$0.00	$0.00	$500.00

Table 24.1.3 What do you expect will be the total value of spending derived from grants in the 2013-14 academic year? Broken out by full-time equivalent enrollment of the college.

Enrollment	Mean	Median	Minimum	Maximum
Less than 2,500	$542.86	$0.00	$0.00	$3,000.00
2,500 to 7,499	$571.43	$0.00	$0.00	$4,000.00
7,500 or more	$916.67	$0.00	$0.00	$5,000.00

Table 24.1.4 What do you expect will be the total value of spending derived from grants in the 2013-14 academic year? Broken out by public or private status of the college.

Public or Private	Mean	Median	Minimum	Maximum
Public	$782.35	$0.00	$0.00	$5,000.00
Private	$0.00	$0.00	$0.00	$0.00

Table 24.1.5 What do you expect will be the total value of spending derived from grants in the 2013-14 academic year? Broken out by annual full-time tuition prior to any deductions.

Tuition	Mean	Median	Minimum	Maximum
Less than $5,000	$380.00	$0.00	$0.00	$3,000.00
$5,000 to $14,999	$1,800.00	$0.00	$0.00	$5,000.00
$15,000 or more	$100.00	$0.00	$0.00	$500.00

Table 25 How much did the library accrue from special endowments in the past year?

Table 25.1.1 How much did the library accrue from special endowments in the past year?

	Mean	Median	Minimum	Maximum
Entire sample	$2,265.79	$0.00	$0.00	$40,000.00

Table 25.1.2 How much did the library accrue from special endowments in the past year? Broken out by type of college.

Type of College	Mean	Median	Minimum	Maximum
Community college	$72.73	$0.00	$0.00	$500.00
4-year BA- or MA-granting college	$10,062.50	$125.00	$0.00	$40,000.00
PhD-granting college or research university	$500.00	$0.00	$0.00	$2,000.00

Table 25.1.3 How much did the library accrue from special endowments in the past year? Broken out by full-time equivalent enrollment of the college.

Enrollment	Mean	Median	Minimum	Maximum
Less than 2,500	$5,757.14	$0.00	$0.00	$40,000.00
2,500 to 7,499	$107.14	$0.00	$0.00	$500.00
7,500 or more	$400.00	$0.00	$0.00	$2,000.00

Table 25.1.4 How much did the library accrue from special endowments in the past year? Broken out by public or private status of the college.

Public or Private	Mean	Median	Minimum	Maximum
Public	$179.41	$0.00	$0.00	$2,000.00
Private	$20,000.00	$20,000.00	$0.00	$40,000.00

Table 25.1.5 How much did the library accrue from special endowments in the past year? Broken out by annual full-time tuition prior to any deductions.

Tuition	Mean	Median	Minimum	Maximum
Less than $5,000	$25.00	$0.00	$0.00	$250.00
$5,000 to $14,999	$160.00	$0.00	$0.00	$500.00
$15,000 or more	$10,500.00	$1,000.00	$0.00	$40,000.00

Chapter 6 – Capital Spending

Table 26 In the past two years, how has the library's capital budget changed?

Table 26.1.1 In the past two years, how has the library's capital budget changed?

	Declined	Remained the same	Increased somewhat	Increased significantly
Entire sample	45.83%	37.50%	12.50%	4.17%

Table 26.1.2 In the past two years, how has the library's capital budget changed? Broken out by type of college.

Type of College	Declined	Remained the same	Increased somewhat	Increased significantly
Community college	45.45%	36.36%	9.09%	9.09%
4-year BA- or MA-granting college	33.33%	66.67%	0.00%	0.00%
PhD-granting college or research university	57.14%	14.29%	28.57%	0.00%

Table 26.1.3 In the past two years, how has the library's capital budget changed? Broken out by full-time equivalent enrollment of the college.

Enrollment	Declined	Remained the same	Increased somewhat	Increased significantly
Less than 2,500	25.00%	62.50%	0.00%	12.50%
2,500 to 7,499	33.33%	44.44%	22.22%	0.00%
7,500 or more	85.71%	0.00%	14.29%	0.00%

Table 26.1.4 In the past two years, how has the library's capital budget changed? Broken out by public or private status of the college.

Public or Private	Declined	Remained the same	Increased somewhat	Increased significantly
Public	52.63%	31.58%	10.53%	5.26%
Private	20.00%	60.00%	20.00%	0.00%

Table 26.1.5 In the past two years, how has the library's capital budget changed? Broken out by annual full-time tuition prior to any deductions.

Tuition	Declined	Remained the same	Increased somewhat	Increased significantly
Less than $5,000	60.00%	30.00%	0.00%	10.00%
$5,000 to $14,999	42.86%	42.86%	14.29%	0.00%
$15,000 or more	28.57%	42.86%	28.57%	0.00%

Table 27 Over the next three years, how do you expect the library's capital budget to change?

Table 27.1.1 Over the next three years, how do you expect the library's capital budget to change?

	Decline	Remain the same	Increase somewhat	Increase significantly
Entire sample	58.33%	33.33%	8.33%	0.00%

Table 27.1.2 Over the next three years, how do you expect the library's capital budget to change? Broken out by type of college.

Type of College	Decline	Remain the same	Increase somewhat	Increase significantly
Community college	63.64%	27.27%	9.09%	0.00%
4-year BA- or MA-granting college	33.33%	66.67%	0.00%	0.00%
PhD-granting college or research university	71.43%	14.29%	14.29%	0.00%

Table 27.1.3 Over the next three years, how do you expect the library's capital budget to change? Broken out by full-time equivalent enrollment of the college.

Enrollment	Decline	Remain the same	Increase somewhat	Increase significantly
Less than 2,500	62.50%	37.50%	0.00%	0.00%
2,500 to 7,499	44.44%	44.44%	11.11%	0.00%
7,500 or more	71.43%	14.29%	14.29%	0.00%

Table 27.1.4 Over the next three years, how do you expect the library's capital budget to change? Broken out by public or private status of the college.

Public or Private	Decline	Remain the same	Increase somewhat	Increase significantly
Public	68.42%	21.05%	10.53%	0.00%
Private	20.00%	80.00%	0.00%	0.00%

Table 27.1.5 Over the next three years, how do you expect the library's capital budget to change? Broken out by annual full-time tuition prior to any deductions.

Tuition	Decline	Remain the same	Increase somewhat	Increase significantly
Less than $5,000	70.00%	30.00%	0.00%	0.00%
$5,000 to $14,999	71.43%	14.29%	14.29%	0.00%
$15,000 or more	28.57%	57.14%	14.29%	0.00%

Table 28 How has capital spending[1] on new library buildings changed over the past three years?

Table 28.1.1 How has capital spending on new library buildings changed over the past three years?

	No Answer	Decreased	Remained the same	Increased somewhat	Increased significantly
Entire sample	70.83%	20.83%	4.17%	0.00%	4.17%

Table 28.1.2 How has capital spending on new library buildings changed over the past three years? Broken out by type of college.

Type of College	No Answer	Decreased	Remained the same	Increased somewhat	Increased significantly
Community college	81.82%	18.18%	0.00%	0.00%	0.00%
4-year BA- or MA-granting college	100.00%	0.00%	0.00%	0.00%	0.00%
PhD-granting college or research university	28.57%	42.86%	14.29%	0.00%	14.29%

---

[1] If spending has been impacted by funds from another source (e.g. grants, special legislative earmarks, and donations or other sources that are not part of the capital budget), you should consider this as part of the capital budget for purposes of this question

Table 28.1.3 How has capital spending on new library buildings changed over the past three years? Broken out by full-time equivalent enrollment of the college.

Enrollment	No Answer	Decreased	Remained the same	Increased somewhat	Increased significantly
Less than 2,500	75.00%	25.00%	0.00%	0.00%	0.00%
2,500 to 7,499	77.78%	11.11%	11.11%	0.00%	0.00%
7,500 or more	57.14%	28.57%	0.00%	0.00%	14.29%

Table 28.1.4 How has capital spending on new library buildings changed over the past three years? Broken out by public or private status of the college.

Public or Private	No Answer	Decreased	Remained the same	Increased somewhat	Increased significantly
Public	73.68%	26.32%	0.00%	0.00%	0.00%
Private	60.00%	0.00%	20.00%	0.00%	20.00%

Table 28.1.5 How has capital spending on new library buildings changed over the past three years? Broken out by annual full-time tuition prior to any deductions.

Tuition	No Answer	Decreased	Remained the same	Increased somewhat	Increased significantly
Less than $5,000	80.00%	20.00%	0.00%	0.00%	0.00%
$5,000 to $14,999	71.43%	28.57%	0.00%	0.00%	0.00%
$15,000 or more	57.14%	14.29%	14.29%	0.00%	14.29%

Table 29 How has capital spending on extensions or significant renovations of existing library buildings changed over the past three years?

Table 29.1.1 How has capital spending on extensions or significant renovations of existing library buildings changed over the past three years?

	No Answer	Decreased	Remained the same	Increased somewhat	Increased significantly
Entire sample	45.83%	25.00%	8.33%	4.17%	16.67%

Table 29.1.2 How has capital spending on extensions or significant renovations of existing library buildings changed over the past three years? Broken out by type of college.

Type of College	No Answer	Decreased	Remained the same	Increased somewhat	Increased significantly
Community college	54.55%	18.18%	9.09%	0.00%	18.18%
4-year BA- or MA-granting college	16.67%	33.33%	16.67%	0.00%	33.33%
PhD-granting college or research university	57.14%	28.57%	0.00%	14.29%	0.00%

Table 29.1.3 How has capital spending on extensions or significant renovations of existing library buildings changed over the past three years? Broken out by full-time equivalent enrollment of the college.

Enrollment	No Answer	Decreased	Remained the same	Increased somewhat	Increased significantly
Less than 2,500	25.00%	37.50%	12.50%	0.00%	25.00%
2,500 to 7,499	55.56%	11.11%	11.11%	11.11%	11.11%
7,500 or more	57.14%	28.57%	0.00%	0.00%	14.29%

Table 29.1.4 How has capital spending on extensions or significant renovations of existing library buildings changed over the past three years? Broken out by public or private status of the college.

Public or Private	No Answer	Decreased	Remained the same	Increased somewhat	Increased significantly
Public	47.37%	21.05%	10.53%	0.00%	21.05%
Private	40.00%	40.00%	0.00%	20.00%	0.00%

Table 29.1.5 How has capital spending on extensions or significant renovations of existing library buildings changed over the past three years? Broken out by annual full-time tuition prior to any deductions.

Tuition	No Answer	Decreased	Remained the same	Increased somewhat	Increased significantly
Less than $5,000	40.00%	20.00%	20.00%	0.00%	20.00%
$5,000 to $14,999	57.14%	14.29%	0.00%	0.00%	28.57%
$15,000 or more	42.86%	42.86%	0.00%	14.29%	0.00%

Table 30 How has capital spending on repairs to library buildings changed over the past three years?

Table 30.1.1 How has capital spending on repairs to library buildings changed over the past three years?

	No Answer	Decreased	Remained the same	Increased somewhat	Increased significantly
Entire sample	45.83%	4.17%	20.83%	29.17%	0.00%

Table 30.1.2 How has capital spending on repairs to library buildings changed over the past three years? Broken out by type of college.

Type of College	No Answer	Decreased	Remained the same	Increased somewhat	Increased significantly
Community college	45.45%	9.09%	18.18%	27.27%	0.00%
4-year BA- or MA-granting college	16.67%	0.00%	33.33%	50.00%	0.00%
PhD-granting college or research university	71.43%	0.00%	14.29%	14.29%	0.00%

Table 30.1.3 How has capital spending on repairs to library buildings changed over the past three years? Broken out by full-time equivalent enrollment of the college.

Enrollment	No Answer	Decreased	Remained the same	Increased somewhat	Increased significantly
Less than 2,500	25.00%	0.00%	12.50%	62.50%	0.00%
2,500 to 7,499	44.44%	11.11%	22.22%	22.22%	0.00%
7,500 or more	71.43%	0.00%	28.57%	0.00%	0.00%

Table 30.1.4 How has capital spending on repairs to library buildings changed over the past three years? Broken out by public or private status of the college.

Public or Private	No Answer	Decreased	Remained the same	Increased somewhat	Increased significantly
Public	47.37%	5.26%	21.05%	26.32%	0.00%
Private	40.00%	0.00%	20.00%	40.00%	0.00%

Table 30.1.5 How has capital spending on repairs to library buildings changed over the past three years? Broken out by annual full-time tuition prior to any deductions.

Tuition	No Answer	Decreased	Remained the same	Increased somewhat	Increased significantly
Less than $5,000	50.00%	10.00%	10.00%	30.00%	0.00%
$5,000 to $14,999	28.57%	0.00%	42.86%	28.57%	0.00%
$15,000 or more	57.14%	0.00%	14.29%	28.57%	0.00%

Table 31 How has capital spending on maintenance of IT equipment stock changed over the past three years?

Table 31.1.1 How has capital spending on maintenance of IT equipment stock changed over the past three years?

	No Answer	Decreased	Remained the same	Increased somewhat	Increased significantly
Entire sample	58.33%	4.17%	25.00%	8.33%	4.17%

Table 31.1.2 How has capital spending on maintenance of IT equipment stock changed over the past three years? Broken out by type of college.

Type of College	No Answer	Decreased	Remained the same	Increased somewhat	Increased significantly
Community college	63.64%	0.00%	27.27%	0.00%	9.09%
4-year BA- or MA-granting college	50.00%	16.67%	16.67%	16.67%	0.00%
PhD-granting college or research university	57.14%	0.00%	28.57%	14.29%	0.00%

Table 31.1.3 How has capital spending on maintenance of IT equipment stock changed over the past three years? Broken out by full-time equivalent enrollment of the college.

Enrollment	No Answer	Decreased	Remained the same	Increased somewhat	Increased significantly
Less than 2,500	62.50%	0.00%	25.00%	0.00%	12.50%
2,500 to 7,499	66.67%	11.11%	22.22%	0.00%	0.00%
7,500 or more	42.86%	0.00%	28.57%	28.57%	0.00%

Table 31.1.4 How has capital spending on maintenance of IT equipment stock changed over the past three years? Broken out by public or private status of the college.

Public or Private	No Answer	Decreased	Remained the same	Increased somewhat	Increased significantly
Public	57.89%	5.26%	21.05%	10.53%	5.26%
Private	60.00%	0.00%	40.00%	0.00%	0.00%

Table 31.1.5 How has capital spending on maintenance of IT equipment stock changed over the past three years? Broken out by annual full-time tuition prior to any deductions.

Tuition	No Answer	Decreased	Remained the same	Increased somewhat	Increased significantly
Less than $5,000	70.00%	0.00%	20.00%	0.00%	10.00%
$5,000 to $14,999	42.86%	14.29%	14.29%	28.57%	0.00%
$15,000 or more	57.14%	0.00%	42.86%	0.00%	0.00%

Table 32 How has capital spending on new IT equipment changed over the past three years?

Table 32.1.1 How has capital spending on new IT equipment changed over the past three years?

	No Answer	Decreased	Remained the same	Increased somewhat	Increased significantly
Entire sample	33.33%	12.50%	29.17%	16.67%	8.33%

Table 32.1.2 How has capital spending on new IT equipment changed over the past three years? Broken out by type of college.

Type of College	No Answer	Decreased	Remained the same	Increased somewhat	Increased significantly
Community college	36.36%	9.09%	27.27%	18.18%	9.09%
4-year BA- or MA-granting college	33.33%	16.67%	16.67%	16.67%	16.67%
PhD-granting college or research university	28.57%	14.29%	42.86%	14.29%	0.00%

Table 32.1.3 How has capital spending on new IT equipment changed over the past three years? Broken out by full-time equivalent enrollment of the college.

Enrollment	No Answer	Decreased	Remained the same	Increased somewhat	Increased significantly
Less than 2,500	25.00%	0.00%	37.50%	25.00%	12.50%
2,500 to 7,499	44.44%	11.11%	22.22%	11.11%	11.11%
7,500 or more	28.57%	28.57%	28.57%	14.29%	0.00%

Table 32.1.4 How has capital spending on new IT equipment changed over the past three years? Broken out by public or private status of the college.

Public or Private	No Answer	Decreased	Remained the same	Increased somewhat	Increased significantly
Public	31.58%	10.53%	36.84%	15.79%	5.26%
Private	40.00%	20.00%	0.00%	20.00%	20.00%

Table 32.1.5 How has capital spending on new IT equipment changed over the past three years? Broken out by annual full-time tuition prior to any deductions.

Tuition	No Answer	Decreased	Remained the same	Increased somewhat	Increased significantly
Less than $5,000	40.00%	10.00%	30.00%	20.00%	0.00%
$5,000 to $14,999	28.57%	14.29%	42.86%	0.00%	14.29%
$15,000 or more	28.57%	14.29%	14.29%	28.57%	14.29%

Chapter 7 – Technology Education Center

Table 33 How much has the library spent over the past three years to develop new library instructional centers or to re-equip/upgrade existing ones with new computers, workstations, or other technology?

Table 33.1.1 How much has the library spent over the past three years to develop new library instructional centers or to re-equip/upgrade existing ones with new computers, workstations, or other technology?

	Mean	Median	Minimum	Maximum
Entire sample	$340,785.00	$0.00	$0.00	$6,685,200.00

Table 33.1.2 How much has the library spent over the past three years to develop new library instructional centers or to re-equip/upgrade existing ones with new computers, workstations, or other technology? Broken out by type of college.

Type of College	Mean	Median	Minimum	Maximum
Community college	$6,681.82	$0.00	$0.00	$50,000.00
4-year BA- or MA-granting college	$14,250.00	$3,500.00	$0.00	$50,000.00
PhD-granting college or research university	$1,337,040.00	$0.00	$0.00	$6,685,200.00

Table 33.1.3 How much has the library spent over the past three years to develop new library instructional centers or to re-equip/upgrade existing ones with new computers, workstations, or other technology? Broken out by full-time equivalent enrollment of the college.

Enrollment	Mean	Median	Minimum	Maximum
Less than 2,500	$9,571.43	$2,000.00	$0.00	$50,000.00
2,500 to 7,499	$836,087.50	$0.00	$0.00	$6,685,200.00
7,500 or more	$12,000.00	$0.00	$0.00	$50,000.00

Table 33.1.4 How much has the library spent over the past three years to develop new library instructional centers or to re-equip/upgrade existing ones with new computers, workstations, or other technology? Broken out by public or private status of the college.

Public or Private	Mean	Median	Minimum	Maximum
Public	$400,511.76	$0.00	$0.00	$6,685,200.00
Private	$2,333.33	$2,000.00	$0.00	$5,000.00

Table 33.1.5 How much has the library spent over the past three years to develop new library instructional centers or to re-equip/upgrade existing ones with new computers, workstations, or other technology? Broken out by annual full-time tuition prior to any deductions.

Tuition	Mean	Median	Minimum	Maximum
Less than $5,000	$7,350.00	$0.00	$0.00	$50,000.00
$5,000 to $14,999	$1,347,040.00	$0.00	$0.00	$6,685,200.00
$15,000 or more	$1,400.00	$0.00	$0.00	$5,000.00

If your library plays a role in the student retention efforts of your college, explain this role, including what services, technologies, and approaches you have found effective, as well as your plans for the future.

1. Writing support.

2. We feel that we have an impact on student retention but have not developed tools to measure this.

3. We are working on this question but have no answers presently.

4. Added a new information commons to provide spaces for collaboration and use of new technologies.

5. Creating a welcoming environment where students feel valued allows them to return when help is needed for completion of research assignments. Quiet study space is critical for our commuter students.

6. We have developed unique tools -- tutorials, assignment calculator, online research game -- to support students.

7. We have just begun to participate in our FYE program.

8. I teach research methods to all classes who will allow me in using the applicable databases and resources. Students use the libraries computers to research their topics and I help them.

9. Going to student recruitment nights, involvement across campus, involvement in first year experiences, new library commons and 24 hour study space. Creating more partnerships and relationships with students.

10. We do play a role, but it is more passive. We try to support these efforts by doing more with our space (hosting tutoring sessions, having Adviser training sessions in the Library) and by providing either man-power or research-support for initiatives.

11. Via our information literacy programme and via content development in the VLE.

12. We provide the information sources necessary for college success.

13. We participate in student orientations and other student related activities. We have LibAnswers, LibCal, LibGuides CMS and products that make

research easier. Problems with research are a significant problem with retention. We also work with Distance Learning and the Learning Center to promote our services. We intend to investigate other best practices to get ideas for the future.

14. Improved student social areas within the libraries, outreach work with local state schools and colleges, specialised student support services.

15. Library provides support to student success efforts. Library chaired campus student success committee. Students in Introduction to the university course were givien library instruction.

16. Not directly involved; do host study tables for athletes esp. after hours.

Chapter 8 – Books

Table 34 How much did the library spend on traditional print books in the 2013-14 academic year?

Table 34.1.1 How much did the library spend on traditional print books in the 2013-14 academic year?

	Mean	Median	Minimum	Maximum
Entire sample	$82,343.25	$37,500.00	$2,700.00	$439,551.00

Table 34.1.2 How much did the library spend on traditional print books in the 2013-14 academic year? Broken out by type of college.

Type of College	Mean	Median	Minimum	Maximum
Community college	$32,464.20	$23,000.00	$4,000.00	$101,642.00
4-year BA- or MA-granting college	$62,994.40	$74,972.00	$25,000.00	$100,000.00
PhD-granting college or research university	$201,450.20	$190,000.00	$2,700.00	$439,551.00

Table 34.1.3 How much did the library spend on traditional print books in the 2013-14 academic year? Broken out by full-time equivalent enrollment of the college.

Enrollment	Mean	Median	Minimum	Maximum
Less than 2,500	$26,709.00	$22,500.00	$2,700.00	$74,972.00
2,500 to 7,499	$65,857.14	$35,000.00	$15,000.00	$190,000.00
7,500 or more	$194,438.60	$101,642.00	$56,000.00	$439,551.00

Table 34.1.4 How much did the library spend on traditional print books in the 2013-14 academic year? Broken out by public or private status of the college.

Public or Private	Mean	Median	Minimum	Maximum
Public	$89,493.31	$33,500.00	$2,700.00	$439,551.00
Private	$53,743.00	$57,486.00	$25,000.00	$75,000.00

Table 34.1.5 How much did the library spend on traditional print books in the 2013-14 academic year? Broken out by annual full-time tuition prior to any deductions.

Tuition	Mean	Median	Minimum	Maximum
Less than $5,000	$37,371.33	$20,000.00	$2,700.00	$101,642.00
$5,000 to $14,999	$71,200.00	$35,000.00	$24,000.00	$190,000.00
$15,000 or more	$159,087.17	$74,986.00	$25,000.00	$439,551.00

Table 35 How much do you expect the library to spend on print books in the 2014-15 academic year?

Table 35.1.1 How much do you expect the library to spend on print books in the 2014-15 academic year?

	Mean	Median	Minimum	Maximum
Entire sample	$77,767.65	$35,000.00	$0.00	$417,825.00

Table 35.1.2 How much do you expect the library to spend on print books in the 2014-15 academic year? Broken out by type of college.

Type of College	Mean	Median	Minimum	Maximum
Community college	$29,700.00	$24,500.00	$4,000.00	$98,000.00
4-year BA- or MA-granting college	$65,000.00	$75,000.00	$25,000.00	$100,000.00
PhD-granting college or research university	$186,670.60	$190,528.00	$0.00	$417,825.00

Table 35.1.3 How much do you expect the library to spend on print books in the 2014-15 academic year? Broken out by full-time equivalent enrollment of the college.

Enrollment	Mean	Median	Minimum	Maximum
Less than 2,500	$27,250.00	$25,000.00	$0.00	$85,000.00
2,500 to 7,499	$63,789.71	$25,000.00	$15,000.00	$190,528.00
7,500 or more	$178,165.00	$98,000.00	$50,000.00	$417,825.00

Table 35.1.4 How much do you expect the library to spend on print books in the 2014-15 academic year? Broken out by public or private status of the college.

Public or Private	Mean	Median	Minimum	Maximum
Public	$83,147.06	$27,500.00	$0.00	$417,825.00
Private	$56,250.00	$57,500.00	$25,000.00	$85,000.00

Table 35.1.5 How much do you expect the library to spend on print books in the 2014-15 academic year? Broken out by annual full-time tuition prior to any deductions.

Tuition	Mean	Median	Minimum	Maximum
Less than $5,000	$35,333.33	$17,000.00	$0.00	$100,000.00
$5,000 to $14,999	$68,905.60	$30,000.00	$24,000.00	$190,528.00
$15,000 or more	$148,804.17	$80,000.00	$25,000.00	$417,825.00

Table 36 How much did the library spend on subscribing to or purchasing e-books in the 2012-13 academic year?

Table 36.1.1 How much did the library spend on subscribing to or purchasing e-books in the 2012-13 academic year?

	Mean	Median	Minimum	Maximum
Entire sample	$9,696.38	$3,750.00	$0.00	$40,542.00

Table 36.1.2 How much did the library spend on subscribing to or purchasing e-books in the 2012-13 academic year? Broken out by type of college.

Type of College	Mean	Median	Minimum	Maximum
Community college	$4,400.00	$2,500.00	$0.00	$15,000.00
4-year BA- or MA-granting college	$25,135.50	$30,000.00	$0.00	$40,542.00
PhD-granting college or research university	$5,000.00	$5,000.00	$0.00	$10,000.00

Table 36.1.3 How much did the library spend on subscribing to or purchasing e-books in the 2012-13 academic year? Broken out by full-time equivalent enrollment of the college.

Enrollment	Mean	Median	Minimum	Maximum
Less than 2,500	$8,455.25	$1,300.00	$0.00	$40,542.00
2,500 to 7,499	$4,500.00	$3,000.00	$2,000.00	$10,000.00
7,500 or more	$21,666.67	$15,000.00	$10,000.00	$40,000.00

Table 36.1.4 How much did the library spend on subscribing to or purchasing e-books in the 2012-13 academic year? Broken out by public or private status of the college.

Public or Private	Mean	Median	Minimum	Maximum
Public	$7,466.67	$2,750.00	$0.00	$40,000.00
Private	$16,385.50	$1,2500.00	$0.00	$40,542.00

Table 36.1.5 How much did the library spend on subscribing to or purchasing e-books in the 2012-13 academic year? Broken out by annual full-time tuition prior to any deductions.

Tuition	Mean	Median	Minimum	Maximum
Less than $5,000	$3,585.71	$2,000.00	$0.00	$15,000.00
$5,000 to $14,999	$13,625.00	$6,250.00	$2,000.00	$40,000.00
$15,000 or more	$15,108.40	$10,000.00	$0.00	$40,542.00

Table 37 How much did the library spend on subscribing to or purchasing e-books in the 2013-14 academic year?

Table 37.1.1 How much did the library spend on subscribing to or purchasing e-books in the 2013-14 academic year?

	Mean	Median	Minimum	Maximum
Entire sample	$11,765.94	$6,000.00	$0.00	$47,755.00

Table 37.1.2 How much did the library spend on subscribing to or purchasing e-books in the 2013-14 academic year? Broken out by type of college.

Type of College	Mean	Median	Minimum	Maximum
Community college	$5,611.11	$5,000.00	$800.00	$20,000.00
4-year BA- or MA-granting college	$26,938.75	$30,000.00	$0.00	$47,755.00
PhD-granting college or research university	$10,000.00	$15,000.00	$0.00	$15,000.00

Table 37.1.3 How much did the library spend on subscribing to or purchasing e-books in the 2013-14 academic year? Broken out by full-time equivalent enrollment of the college.

Enrollment	Mean	Median	Minimum	Maximum
Less than 2,500	$12,219.38	$1,600.00	$0.00	$47,755.00
2,500 to 7,499	$7,100.00	$6,000.00	$2,500.00	$15,000.00
7,500 or more	$18,333.33	$20,000.00	$15,000.00	$20,000.00

Table 37.1.4 How much did the library spend on subscribing to or purchasing e-books in the 2013-14 academic year? Broken out by public or private status of the college.

Public or Private	Mean	Median	Minimum	Maximum
Public	$7,125.00	$5,500.00	$0.00	$20,000.00
Private	$25,688.75	$27,500.00	$0.00	$47,755.00

Table 37.1.5 How much did the library spend on subscribing to or purchasing e-books in the 2013-14 academic year? Broken out by annual full-time tuition prior to any deductions.

Tuition	Mean	Median	Minimum	Maximum
Less than $5,000	$5,857.14	$6,000.00	$0.00	$20,000.00
$5,000 to $14,999	$7,375.00	$3,750.00	$2,000.00	$20,000.00
$15,000 or more	$23,551.00	$15,000.00	$0.00	$47,755.00

Table 38 How much do you expect the library to spend on subscribing to or purchasing e-books in the 2014-15 academic year?

Table 38.1.1 How much do you expect the library to spend on subscribing to or purchasing e-books in the 2014-15 academic year?

	Mean	Median	Minimum	Maximum
Entire sample	$12,843.75	$6,750.00	$0.00	$55,000.00

Table 38.1.2 How much do you expect the library to spend on subscribing to or purchasing e-books in the 2014-15 academic year? Broken out by type of college.

Type of College	Mean	Median	Minimum	Maximum
Community college	$6,166.67	$5,000.00	$2,000.00	$20,000.00
4-year BA- or MA-granting college	$28,750.00	$30,000.00	$0.00	$55,000.00
PhD-granting college or research university	$11,666.67	$15,000.00	$0.00	$20,000.00

Table 38.1.3 How much do you expect the library to spend on subscribing to or purchasing e-books in the 2014-15 academic year? Broken out by full-time equivalent enrollment of the college.

Enrollment	Mean	Median	Minimum	Maximum
Less than 2,500	$13,687.50	$2,250.00	$0.00	$55,000.00
2,500 to 7,499	$8,200.00	$6,500.00	$2,500.00	$20,000.00
7,500 or more	$18,333.33	$20,000.00	$15,000.00	$20,000.00

Table 38.1.4 How much do you expect the library to spend on subscribing to or purchasing e-books in the 2014-15 academic year? Broken out by public or private status of the college.

Public or Private	Mean	Median	Minimum	Maximum
Public	$7,541.67	$5,750.00	$0.00	$20,000.00
Private	$28,750.00	$30,000.00	$0.00	$55,000.00

Table 38.1.5 How much do you expect the library to spend on subscribing to or purchasing e-books in the 2014-15 academic year? Broken out by annual full-time tuition prior to any deductions.

Tuition	Mean	Median	Minimum	Maximum
Less than $5,000	$6,571.43	$6,500.00	$0.00	$20,000.00
$5,000 to $14,999	$7,375.00	$3,750.00	$2,000.00	$20,000.00
$15,000 or more	$26,000.00	$20,000.00	$0.00	$55,000.00

Table 39 What was the library's total spending on books or other intellectual property with Amazon in the 2012-13 academic year?

Table 39.1.1 What was the library's total spending on books or other intellectual property with Amazon in the 2012-13 academic year?

	Mean	Median	Minimum	Maximum
Entire sample	$9,060.67	$3,000.00	$0.00	$50,000.00

Table 39.1.2 What was the library's total spending on books or other intellectual property with Amazon in the 2012-13 academic year? Broken out by type of college.

Type of College	Mean	Median	Minimum	Maximum
Community college	$6,010.71	$1,575.00	$0.00	$30,000.00
4-year BA- or MA-granting college	$13,333.33	$10,000.00	$5,000.00	$25,000.00
PhD-granting college or research university	$10,767.00	$835.00	$0.00	$50,000.00

Table 39.1.3 What was the library's total spending on books or other intellectual property with Amazon in the 2012-13 academic year? Broken out by full-time equivalent enrollment of the college.

Enrollment	Mean	Median	Minimum	Maximum
Less than 2,500	$2,439.29	$500.00	$0.00	$10,000.00
2,500 to 7,499	$3,250.00	$4,000.00	$0.00	$5,000.00
7,500 or more	$26,458.75	$27,500.00	$835.00	$50,000.00

Table 39.1.4 What was the library's total spending on books or other intellectual property with Amazon in the 2012-13 academic year? Broken out by public or private status of the college.

Public or Private	Mean	Median	Minimum	Maximum
Public	$9,825.83	$1,205.00	$0.00	$50,000.00
Private	$6,000.00	$5,000.00	$3,000.00	$10,000.00

Table 39.1.5 What was the library's total spending on books or other intellectual property with Amazon in the 2012-13 academic year? Broken out by annual full-time tuition prior to any deductions.

Tuition	Mean	Median	Minimum	Maximum
Less than $5,000	$6,095.83	$787.50	$0.00	$30,000.00
$5,000 to $14,999	$7,625.00	$2,750.00	$0.00	$25,000.00
$15,000 or more	$13,767.00	$5,000.00	$835.00	$50,000.00

Table 40 What was the library's total spending on books or other intellectual property with Alibris in the 2012-13 academic year?

Table 40.1.1 What was the library's total spending on books or other intellectual property with Alibris in the 2012-13 academic year?

	Mean	Median	Minimum	Maximum
Entire sample	$5,016.67	$0.00	$0.00	$75,000.00

Table 40.1.2 What was the library's total spending on books or other intellectual property with Alibris in the 2012-13 academic year? Broken out by type of college.

Type of College	Mean	Median	Minimum	Maximum
Community college	$0.00	$0.00	$0.00	$0.00
4-year BA- or MA-granting college	$0.00	$0.00	$0.00	$0.00
PhD-granting college or research university	$15,050.00	$0.00	$0.00	$75,000.00

Table 40.1.3 What was the library's total spending on books or other intellectual property with Alibris in the 2012-13 academic year? Broken out by full-time equivalent enrollment of the college.

Enrollment	Mean	Median	Minimum	Maximum
Less than 2,500	$0.00	$0.00	$0.00	$0.00
2,500 to 7,499	$62.50	$0.00	$0.00	$250.00
7,500 or more	$18,750.00	$0.00	$0.00	$75,000.00

Table 40.1.4 What was the library's total spending on books or other intellectual property with Alibris in the 2012-13 academic year? Broken out by public or private status of the college.

Public or Private	Mean	Median	Minimum	Maximum
Public	$6,250.00	$0.00	$0.00	$75,000.00
Private	$83.33	$0.00	$0.00	$250.00

Table 40.1.5 What was the library's total spending on books or other intellectual property with Alibris in the 2012-13 academic year? Broken out by annual full-time tuition prior to any deductions.

Tuition	Mean	Median	Minimum	Maximum
Less than $5,000	$0.00	$0.00	$0.00	$0.00
$5,000 to $14,999	$0.00	$0.00	$0.00	$0.00
$15,000 or more	$15,050.00	$0.00	$0.00	$75,000.00

Table 41 What was the library's total spending on books or other intellectual property with Barnes & Noble in the 2012-13 academic year?

Table 41.1.1 What was the library's total spending on books or other intellectual property with Barnes & Noble in the 2012-13 academic year?

	Mean	Median	Minimum	Maximum
Entire sample	$5,073.33	$0.00	$0.00	$56,000.00

Table 41.1.2 What was the library's total spending on books or other intellectual property with Barnes & Noble in the 2012-13 academic year? Broken out by type of college.

Type of College	Mean	Median	Minimum	Maximum
Community college	$8,000.00	$0.00	$0.00	$56,000.00
4-year BA- or MA-granting college	$6,666.67	$0.00	$0.00	$20,000.00
PhD-granting college or research university	$20.00	$0.00	$0.00	$100.00

Table 41.1.3 What was the library's total spending on books or other intellectual property with Barnes & Noble in the 2012-13 academic year? Broken out by full-time equivalent enrollment of the college.

Enrollment	Mean	Median	Minimum	Maximum
Less than 2,500	$10,857.14	$0.00	$0.00	$56,000.00
2,500 to 7,499	$25.00	$0.00	$0.00	$100.00
7,500 or more	$0.00	$0.00	$0.00	$0.00

Table 41.1.4 What was the library's total spending on books or other intellectual property with Barnes & Noble in the 2012-13 academic year? Broken out by public or private status of the college.

Public or Private	Mean	Median	Minimum	Maximum
Public	$4,666.67	$0.00	$0.00	$56,000.00
Private	$6,700.00	$100.00	$0.00	$20,000.00

Table 41.1.5 What was the library's total spending on books or other intellectual property with Barnes & Noble in the 2012-13 academic year? Broken out by annual full-time tuition prior to any deductions.

Tuition	Mean	Median	Minimum	Maximum
Less than $5,000	$9,333.33	$0.00	$0.00	$56,000.00
$5,000 to $14,999	$0.00	$0.00	$0.00	$0.00
$15,000 or more	$4,020.00	$0.00	$0.00	$20,000.00

Table 42 What was the library's total spending on books or other intellectual property with Powell's Books in the 2012-13 academic year?

Table 42.1.1 What was the library's total spending on books or other intellectual property with Powell's Books in the 2012-13 academic year?

	Mean	Median	Minimum	Maximum
Entire sample	$13.33	$0.00	$0.00	$200.00

Table 42.1.2 What was the library's total spending on books or other intellectual property with Powell's Books in the 2012-13 academic year? Broken out by type of college.

Type of College	Mean	Median	Minimum	Maximum
Community college	$0.00	$0.00	$0.00	$0.00
4-year BA- or MA-granting college	$0.00	$0.00	$0.00	$0.00
PhD-granting college or research university	$40.00	$0.00	$0.00	$200.00

Table 42.1.3 What was the library's total spending on books or other intellectual property with Powell's Books in the 2012-13 academic year? Broken out by full-time equivalent enrollment of the college.

Enrollment	Mean	Median	Minimum	Maximum
Less than 2,500	$0.00	$0.00	$0.00	$0.00
2,500 to 7,499	$50.00	$0.00	$0.00	$200.00
7,500 or more	$0.00	$0.00	$0.00	$0.00

Table 42.1.4 What was the library's total spending on books or other intellectual property with Powell's Books in the 2012-13 academic year? Broken out by public or private status of the college.

Public or Private	Mean	Median	Minimum	Maximum
Public	$0.00	$0.00	$0.00	$0.00
Private	$66.67	$0.00	$0.00	$200.00

Table 42.1.5 What was the library's total spending on books or other intellectual property with Powell's Books in the 2012-13 academic year? Broken out by annual full-time tuition prior to any deductions.

Tuition	Mean	Median	Minimum	Maximum
Less than $5,000	$0.00	$0.00	$0.00	$0.00
$5,000 to $14,999	$0.00	$0.00	$0.00	$0.00
$15,000 or more	$40.00	$0.00	$0.00	$200.00

Table 43 What was the library's total spending on books or other intellectual property with Books-A-Million in the 2012-13 academic year?

Table 43.1.1 What was the library's total spending on books or other intellectual property with Books-A-Million in the 2012-13 academic year?

	Mean	Median	Minimum	Maximum
Entire sample	$0.00	$0.00	$0.00	$0.00

Table 44 What was the library's total spending on books or other intellectual property with all other online booksellers in the 2012-13 academic year?

Table 44.1.1 What was the library's total spending on books or other intellectual property with all other online booksellers in the 2012-13 academic year?

	Mean	Median	Minimum	Maximum
Entire sample	$17,258.33	$675.00	$0.00	$175,000.00

Table 44.1.2 What was the library's total spending on books or other intellectual property with all other online booksellers in the 2012-13 academic year? Broken out by type of college.

Type of College	Mean	Median	Minimum	Maximum
Community college	$3,525.00	$0.00	$0.00	$20,000.00
4-year BA- or MA-granting college	$18,333.33	$5,000.00	$0.00	$50,000.00
PhD-granting college or research university	$35,840.00	$1,500.00	$0.00	$175,000.00

Table 44.1.3 What was the library's total spending on books or other intellectual property with all other online booksellers in the 2012-13 academic year? Broken out by full-time equivalent enrollment of the college.

Enrollment	Mean	Median	Minimum	Maximum
Less than 2,500	$1,767.86	$675.00	$0.00	$5,000.00
2,500 to 7,499	$375.00	$0.00	$0.00	$1,500.00
7,500 or more	$61,250.00	$35,000.00	$0.00	$175,000.00

Table 44.1.4 What was the library's total spending on books or other intellectual property with all other online booksellers in the 2012-13 academic year? Broken out by public or private status of the college.

Public or Private	Mean	Median	Minimum	Maximum
Public	$21,031.25	$337.50	$0.00	$175,000.00
Private	$2,166.67	$1,500.00	$0.00	$5,000.00

Table 44.1.5 What was the library's total spending on books or other intellectual property with all other online booksellers in the 2012-13 academic year? Broken out by annual full-time tuition prior to any deductions.

Tuition	Mean	Median	Minimum	Maximum
Less than $5,000	$4,562.50	$1,687.50	$0.00	$20,000.00
$5,000 to $14,999	$12,500.00	$0.00	$0.00	$50,000.00
$15,000 or more	$36,300.00	$1,500.00	$0.00	$175,000.00

Table 45 What was the library's total spending (including all online booksellers) on books or other intellectual property in the 2012-13 academic year?

Table 45.1.1 What was the library's total spending (including all online booksellers) on books or other intellectual property in the 2012-13 academic year?

	Mean	Median	Minimum	Maximum
Entire sample	$36,885.67	$5,000.00	$0.00	$300,000.00

Table 45.1.2 What was the library's total spending (including all online booksellers) on books or other intellectual property in the 2012-13 academic year? Broken out by type of college.

Type of College	Mean	Median	Minimum	Maximum
Community college	$17,535.71	$5,000.00	$500.00	$56,000.00
4-year BA- or MA-granting college	$38,333.33	$25,000.00	$15,000.00	$75,000.00
PhD-granting college or research university	$63,107.00	$2,700.00	$0.00	$300,000.00

Table 45.1.3 What was the library's total spending (including all online booksellers) on books or other intellectual property in the 2012-13 academic year? Broken out by full-time equivalent enrollment of the college.

Enrollment	Mean	Median	Minimum	Maximum
Less than 2,500	$15,064.29	$4,000.00	$500.00	$56,000.00
2,500 to 7,499	$5,500.00	$5,000.00	$0.00	$12,000.00
7,500 or more	$106,458.75	$62,500.00	$835.00	$300,000.00

Table 45.1.4 What was the library's total spending (including all online booksellers) on books or other intellectual property in the 2012-13 academic year? Broken out by public or private status of the college.

Public or Private	Mean	Median	Minimum	Maximum
Public	$41,773.75	$4,500.00	$0.00	$300,000.00
Private	$17,333.33	$15,000.00	$12,000.00	$25,000.00

Table 45.1.5 What was the library's total spending (including all online booksellers) on books or other intellectual property in the 2012-13 academic year? Broken out by annual full-time tuition prior to any deductions.

Tuition	Mean	Median	Minimum	Maximum
Less than $5,000	$19,991.67	$4,500.00	$2,250.00	$56,000.00
$5,000 to $14,999	$20,125.00	$2,750.00	$0.00	$75,000.00
$15,000 or more	$70,567.00	$15,000.00	$835.00	$300,000.00

Table 46 Has the library purchased e-book readers, iPads, or any other devices for patrons to read e-books?

Table 46.1.1 Has the library purchased e-book readers, iPads, or any other devices for patrons to read e-books?

	No Answer	Yes	No
Entire sample	4.17%	33.33%	62.50%

Table 46.1.2 Has the library purchased e-book readers, iPads, or any other devices for patrons to read e-books? Broken out by type of college.

Type of College	No Answer	Yes	No
Community college	0.00%	27.27%	72.73%
4-year BA- or MA-granting college	16.67%	50.00%	33.33%
PhD-granting college or research university	0.00%	28.57%	71.43%

Table 46.1.3 Has the library purchased e-book readers, iPads, or any other devices for patrons to read e-books? Broken out by full-time equivalent enrollment of the college.

Enrollment	No Answer	Yes	No
Less than 2,500	12.50%	25.00%	62.50%
2,500 to 7,499	0.00%	33.33%	66.67%
7,500 or more	0.00%	42.86%	57.14%

Table 46.1.4 Has the library purchased e-book readers, iPads, or any other devices for patrons to read e-books? Broken out by public or private status of the college.

Public or Private	No Answer	Yes	No
Public	0.00%	36.84%	63.16%
Private	20.00%	20.00%	60.00%

Table 46.1.5 Has the library purchased e-book readers, iPads, or any other devices for patrons to read e-books? Broken out by annual full-time tuition prior to any deductions.

Tuition	No Answer	Yes	No
Less than $5,000	0.00%	20.00%	80.00%
$5,000 to $14,999	0.00%	57.14%	42.86%
$15,000 or more	14.29%	28.57%	57.14%

Table 47 Over the past two years, how much has the library spent on e-book readers and devices?

Table 47.1.1 Over the past two years, how much has the library spent on e-book readers and devices?

	Mean	Median	Minimum	Maximum
Entire sample	$160.53	$0.00	$0.00	$1,000.00

Table 47.1.2 Over the past two years, how much has the library spent on e-book readers and devices? Broken out by type of college.

Type of College	Mean	Median	Minimum	Maximum
Community college	$235.00	$0.00	$0.00	$1,000.00
4-year BA- or MA-granting college	$75.00	$0.00	$0.00	$300.00
PhD-granting college or research university	$80.00	$0.00	$0.00	$400.00

Table 47.1.3 Over the past two years, how much has the library spent on e-book readers and devices? Broken out by full-time equivalent enrollment of the college.

Enrollment	Mean	Median	Minimum	Maximum
Less than 2,500	$92.86	$0.00	$0.00	$350.00
2,500 to 7,499	$166.67	$0.00	$0.00	$1,000.00
7,500 or more	$233.33	$0.00	$0.00	$1,000.00

Table 47.1.4 Over the past two years, how much has the library spent on e-book readers and devices? Broken out by public or private status of the college.

Public or Private	Mean	Median	Minimum	Maximum
Public	$171.88	$0.00	$0.00	$1,000.00
Private	$100.00	$0.00	$0.00	$300.00

Table 47.1.5 Over the past two years, how much has the library spent on e-book readers and devices? Broken out by annual full-time tuition prior to any deductions.

Tuition	Mean	Median	Minimum	Maximum
Less than $5,000	$150.00	$0.00	$0.00	$1,000.00
$5,000 to $14,999	$200.00	$0.00	$0.00	$1,000.00
$15,000 or more	$140.00	$0.00	$0.00	$400.00

Table 48 Over the past two years, how much has the library spent on books and other content for e-book readers and devices?

Table 48.1.1 Over the past two years, how much has the library spent on books and other content for e-book readers and devices?

	Mean	Median	Minimum	Maximum
Entire sample	$856.58	$0.00	$0.00	$15,000.00

Table 48.1.2 Over the past two years, how much has the library spent on books and other content for e-book readers and devices? Broken out by type of college.

Type of College	Mean	Median	Minimum	Maximum
Community college	$107.50	$0.00	$0.00	$1,000.00
4-year BA- or MA-granting college	$50.00	$0.00	$0.00	$200.00
PhD-granting college or research university	$3,000.00	$0.00	$0.00	$15,000.00

Table 48.1.3 Over the past two years, how much has the library spent on books and other content for e-book readers and devices? Broken out by full-time equivalent enrollment of the college.

Enrollment	Mean	Median	Minimum	Maximum
Less than 2,500	$39.29	$0.00	$0.00	$200.00
2,500 to 7,499	$1,66.67	$0.00	$0.00	$1,000.00
7,500 or more	$2,500.00	$0.00	$0.00	$15,000.00

Table 48.1.4 Over the past two years, how much has the library spent on books and other content for e-book readers and devices? Broken out by public or private status of the college.

Public or Private	Mean	Median	Minimum	Maximum
Public	$1,004.69	$0.00	$0.00	$15,000.00
Private	$66.67	$0.00	$0.00	$200.00

Table 48.1.5 Over the past two years, how much has the library spent on books and other content for e-book readers and devices? Broken out by annual full-time tuition prior to any deductions.

Tuition	Mean	Median	Minimum	Maximum
Less than $5,000	$8.33	$0.00	$0.00	$75.00
$5,000 to $14,999	$200.00	$0.00	$0.00	$1,000.00
$15,000 or more	$3,040.00	$0.00	$0.00	$15,000.00

Table 49 Over the past two years, how much has the library spent on software to e-book enable computers or mobile devices?

Table 49.1.1 Over the past two years, how much has the library spent on software to e-book enable computers or mobile devices?

	Mean	Median	Minimum	Maximum
Entire sample	$0.00	$0.00	$0.00	$0.00

Chapter 9 – Journals

Table 50 How much did the library spend on print and electronic subscriptions to scholarly and professional journals in the 2012-13 academic year?

Table 50.1.1 How much did the library spend on print and electronic subscriptions to scholarly and professional journals in the 2012-13 academic year?

	Mean	Median	Minimum	Maximum
Entire sample	$341,186.37	$42,000.00	$800.00	$3,000,000.00

Table 50.1.2 How much did the library spend on print and electronic subscriptions to scholarly and professional journals in the 2012-13 academic year? Broken out by type of college.

Type of College	Mean	Median	Minimum	Maximum
Community college	$11,434.78	$6,000.00	$800.00	$42,000.00
4-year BA- or MA-granting college	$189,424.50	$95,000.00	$50,000.00	$517,698.00
PhD-granting college or research university	$936,988.33	$631,852.00	$3,400.00	$3,000,000.00

Table 50.1.3 How much did the library spend on print and electronic subscriptions to scholarly and professional journals in the 2012-13 academic year? Broken out by full-time equivalent enrollment of the college.

Enrollment	Mean	Median	Minimum	Maximum
Less than 2,500	$85,001.38	$7,000.00	$800.00	$517,698.00
2,500 to 7,499	$71,137.67	$17,000.00	$4,000.00	$200,000.00
7,500 or more	$1,075,140.80	$1,063,704.00	$42,000.00	$3,000,000.00

Table 50.1.4 How much did the library spend on print and electronic subscriptions to scholarly and professional journals in the 2012-13 academic year? Broken out by public or private status of the college.

Public or Private	Mean	Median	Minimum	Maximum
Public	$374,989.53	$8,000.00	$800.00	$3,000,000.00
Private	$214,424.50	$145,000.00	$50,000.00	$517,698.00

Table 50.1.5 How much did the library spend on print and electronic subscriptions to scholarly and professional journals in the 2012-13 academic year? Broken out by annual full-time tuition prior to any deductions.

Tuition	Mean	Median	Minimum	Maximum
Less than $5,000	$9,616.14	$4,113.00	$800.00	$42,000.00
$5,000 to $14,999	$553,971.00	$63,500.00	$4,000.00	$3,000,000.00
$15,000 or more	$515,233.67	$358,849.00	$50,000.00	$1,170,000.00

Table 51 How much did the library spend on print and electronic subscriptions to scholarly and professional journals in the 2013-14 academic year?

Table 51.1.1 How much did the library spend on print and electronic subscriptions to scholarly and professional journals in the 2013-14 academic year?

	Mean	Median	Minimum	Maximum
Entire sample	$359,192.21	$45,000.00	$0.00	$3,200,000.00

Table 51.1.2 How much did the library spend on print and electronic subscriptions to scholarly and professional journals in the 2013-14 academic year? Broken out by type of college.

Type of College	Mean	Median	Minimum	Maximum
Community college	$11,538.89	$6,000.00	$800.00	$45,000.00
4-year BA- or MA-granting college	$203,527.75	$105,000.00	$50,000.00	$554,111.00
PhD-granting college or research university	$984,448.50	$649,438.50	$0.00	$3,200,000.00

Table 51.1.3 How much did the library spend on print and electronic subscriptions to scholarly and professional journals in the 2013-14 academic year? Broken out by full-time equivalent enrollment of the college.

Enrollment	Mean	Median	Minimum	Maximum
Less than 2,500	$88,801.38	$6,500.00	$0.00	$554,111.00
2,500 to 7,499	$81,727.33	$17,250.00	$3,400.00	$240,000.00
7,500 or more	$1,124,775.40	$1,058,877.00	$45,000.00	$3,200,000.00

Table 51.1.4 How much did the library spend on print and electronic subscriptions to scholarly and professional journals in the 2013-14 academic year? Broken out by public or private status of the college.

Public or Private	Mean	Median	Minimum	Maximum
Public	$392,702.73	$7,500.00	$0.00	$3,200,000.00
Private	$233,527.75	$165,000.00	$50,000.00	$554,111.00

Table 51.1.5 How much did the library spend on print and electronic subscriptions to scholarly and professional journals in the 2013-14 academic year? Broken out by annual full-time tuition prior to any deductions.

Tuition	Mean	Median	Minimum	Maximum
Less than $5,000	$9,457.14	$3,400.00	$0.00	$45,000.00
$5,000 to $14,999	$594,244.00	$73,500.00	$4,650.00	$3,200,000.00
$15,000 or more	$532,164.67	$397,055.50	$50,000.00	$1,200,000.00

Table 52 How much does the library expect to spend on print and electronic subscriptions to scholarly and professional journals in the 2014-15 academic year?

Table 52.1.1 How much does the library expect to spend on print and electronic subscriptions to scholarly and professional journals in the 2014-15 academic year?

	Mean	Median	Minimum	Maximum
Entire sample	$379,854.26	$50,000.00	$0.00	$3,500,000.00

Table 52.1.2 How much does the library expect to spend on print and electronic subscriptions to scholarly and professional journals in the 2014-15 academic year? Broken out by type of college.

Type of College	Mean	Median	Minimum	Maximum
Community college	$12,244.44	$5,000.00	$800.00	$50,000.00
4-year BA- or MA-granting college	$208,250.00	$105,000.00	$60,000.00	$563,000.00
PhD-granting college or research university	$104,5671.83	$673,368.00	$0.00	$3,500,000.00

Table 52.1.3 How much does the library expect to spend on print and electronic subscriptions to scholarly and professional journals in the 2014-15 academic year? Broken out by full-time equivalent enrollment of the college.

Enrollment	Mean	Median	Minimum	Maximum
Less than 2,500	$91,475.00	$8,000.00	$0.00	$563,000.00
2,500 to 7,499	$90,615.83	$16,750.00	$3,100.00	$285,000.00
7,500 or more	$1,188,347.20	$1,061,736.00	$50,000.00	$3,500,000.00

Table 52.1.4 How much does the library expect to spend on print and electronic subscriptions to scholarly and professional journals in the 2014-15 academic year? Broken out by public or private status of the college.

Public or Private	Mean	Median	Minimum	Maximum
Public	$414,615.40	$11,000.00	$0.00	$3,500,000.00
Private	$249,500.00	$187,500.00	$60,000.00	$563,000.00

Table 52.1.5 How much does the library expect to spend on print and electronic subscriptions to scholarly and professional journals in the 2014-15 academic year? Broken out by annual full-time tuition prior to any deductions.

Tuition	Mean	Median	Minimum	Maximum
Less than $5,000	$10,485.71	$3,100.00	$0.00	$50,000.00
$5,000 to $14,999	$645,682.50	$73,500.00	$4,800.00	$3,500,000.00
$15,000 or more	$544,956.00	$424,000.00	$60,000.00	$1,210,000.00

Table 53 Approximately what percentage of the library's total spending on scientific and professional journals was dedicated to print subscriptions only?

Table 53.1.1 Approximately what percentage of the library's total spending on scientific and professional journals was dedicated to print subscriptions only?

	Mean	Median	Minimum	Maximum
Entire sample	34.11%	15.00%	3.00%	100.00%

Table 53.1.2 Approximately what percentage of the library's total spending on scientific and professional journals was dedicated to print subscriptions only? Broken out by type of college.

Type of College	Mean	Median	Minimum	Maximum
Community college	48.75%	50.00%	5.00%	100.00%
4-year BA- or MA-granting college	16.83%	13.75%	6.50%	33.33%
PhD-granting college or research university	25.75%	10.50%	3.00%	79.00%

Table 53.1.3 Approximately what percentage of the library's total spending on scientific and professional journals was dedicated to print subscriptions only? Broken out by full-time equivalent enrollment of the college.

Enrollment	Mean	Median	Minimum	Maximum
Less than 2,500	44.30%	33.33%	6.50%	100.00%
2,500 to 7,499	26.40%	14.00%	3.00%	60.00%
7,500 or more	23.17%	12.50%	7.00%	50.00%

Table 53.1.4 Approximately what percentage of the library's total spending on scientific and professional journals was dedicated to print subscriptions only? Broken out by public or private status of the college.

Public or Private	Mean	Median	Minimum	Maximum
Public	40.25%	50.00%	3.00%	100.00%
Private	17.21%	14.50%	6.50%	33.33%

Table 53.1.5 Approximately what percentage of the library's total spending on scientific and professional journals was dedicated to print subscriptions only? Broken out by annual full-time tuition prior to any deductions.

Tuition	Mean	Median	Minimum	Maximum
Less than $5,000	51.05%	50.00%	7.50%	79.00%
$5,000 to $14,999	36.10%	12.50%	3.00%	100.00%
$15,000 or more	15.17%	14.00%	6.50%	33.33%

Table 54 Approximately what percentage of the library's total spending on scientific and professional journals was dedicated to subscriptions with electronic access only?

Table 54.1.1 Approximately what percentage of the library's total spending on scientific and professional journals was dedicated to subscriptions with electronic access only?

	Mean	Median	Minimum	Maximum
Entire sample	43.96%	43.50%	0.00%	91.50%

Table 54.1.2 Approximately what percentage of the library's total spending on scientific and professional journals was dedicated to subscriptions with electronic access only? Broken out by type of college.

Type of College	Mean	Median	Minimum	Maximum
Community college	34.25%	31.25%	0.00%	88.50%
4-year BA- or MA-granting college	66.54%	68.84%	43.50%	85.00%
PhD-granting college or research university	38.38%	31.00%	0.00%	91.50%

Table 54.1.3 Approximately what percentage of the library's total spending on scientific and professional journals was dedicated to subscriptions with electronic access only? Broken out by full-time equivalent enrollment of the college.

Enrollment	Mean	Median	Minimum	Maximum
Less than 2,500	44.99%	43.50%	0.00%	88.50%
2,500 to 7,499	36.40%	40.00%	0.00%	80.00%
7,500 or more	54.17%	71.00%	0.00%	91.50%

Table 54.1.4 Approximately what percentage of the library's total spending on scientific and professional journals was dedicated to subscriptions with electronic access only? Broken out by public or private status of the college.

Public or Private	Mean	Median	Minimum	Maximum
Public	37.02%	31.25%	0.00%	91.50%
Private	63.04%	61.84%	43.50%	85.00%

Table 54.1.5 Approximately what percentage of the library's total spending on scientific and professional journals was dedicated to subscriptions with electronic access only? Broken out by annual full-time tuition prior to any deductions.

Tuition	Mean	Median	Minimum	Maximum
Less than $5,000	23.95%	0.00%	0.00%	88.50%
$5,000 to $14,999	39.20%	40.00%	0.00%	80.00%
$15,000 or more	68.73%	66.67%	43.50%	91.50%

Table 55 Approximately what percentage of the library's total spending on scientific and professional journals was dedicated to subscriptions with both print and electronic access?

Table 55.1.1 Approximately what percentage of the library's total spending on scientific and professional journals was dedicated to subscriptions with both print and electronic access?

	Mean	Median	Minimum	Maximum
Entire sample	21.93%	15.00%	0.00%	92.00%

Table 55.1.2 Approximately what percentage of the library's total spending on scientific and professional journals was dedicated to subscriptions with both print and electronic access? Broken out by type of college.

Type of College	Mean	Median	Minimum	Maximum
Community college	17.00%	4.00%	0.00%	50.00%
4-year BA- or MA-granting college	16.63%	8.25%	0.00%	50.00%
PhD-granting college or research university	35.88%	25.00%	1.50%	92.00%

Table 55.1.3 Approximately what percentage of the library's total spending on scientific and professional journals was dedicated to subscriptions with both print and electronic access? Broken out by full-time equivalent enrollment of the college.

Enrollment	Mean	Median	Minimum	Maximum
Less than 2,500	10.71%	0.00%	0.00%	50.00%
2,500 to 7,499	37.20%	29.00%	0.00%	92.00%
7,500 or more	22.67%	16.50%	1.50%	50.00%

Table 55.1.4 Approximately what percentage of the library's total spending on scientific and professional journals was dedicated to subscriptions with both print and electronic access? Broken out by public or private status of the college.

Public or Private	Mean	Median	Minimum	Maximum
Public	22.73%	15.00%	0.00%	92.00%
Private	19.75%	14.50%	0.00%	50.00%

Table 55.1.5 Approximately what percentage of the library's total spending on scientific and professional journals was dedicated to subscriptions with both print and electronic access? Broken out by annual full-time tuition prior to any deductions.

Tuition	Mean	Median	Minimum	Maximum
Less than $5,000	25.00%	21.00%	0.00%	50.00%
$5,000 to $14,999	24.70%	15.00%	0.00%	92.00%
$15,000 or more	16.10%	1.50%	0.00%	50.00%

Chapter 10 – Special Collections

Table 56 What is the library's aggregated overall budget for its special collections division (or the departments that would fall under such a characterization)?

Table 56.1.1 What is the library's aggregated overall budget for its special collections division (or the departments that would fall under such a characterization)?

	Mean	Median	Minimum	Maximum
Entire sample	$541.88	$0.00	$0.00	$5,000.00

Table 56.1.2 What is the library's aggregated overall budget for its special collections division (or the departments that would fall under such a characterization)? Broken out by type of college.

Type of College	Mean	Median	Minimum	Maximum
Community college	$55.56	$0.00	$0.00	$500.00
4-year BA- or MA-granting college	$1,750.00	$1,000.00	$0.00	$5,000.00
PhD-granting college or research university	$390.00	$0.00	$0.00	$1,170.00

Table 56.1.3 What is the library's aggregated overall budget for its special collections division (or the departments that would fall under such a characterization)? Broken out by full-time equivalent enrollment of the college.

Enrollment	Mean	Median	Minimum	Maximum
Less than 2,500	$875.00	$0.00	$0.00	$5,000.00
2,500 to 7,499	$100.00	$0.00	$0.00	$500.00
7,500 or more	$390.00	$0.00	$0.00	$1,170.00

Table 56.1.4 What is the library's aggregated overall budget for its special collections division (or the departments that would fall under such a characterization)? Broken out by public or private status of the college.

Public or Private	Mean	Median	Minimum	Maximum
Public	$128.46	$0.00	$0.00	$1,170.00
Private	$2,333.33	$2,000.00	$0.00	$5,000.00

Table 56.1.5 What is the library's aggregated overall budget for its special collections division (or the departments that would fall under such a characterization)? Broken out by annual full-time tuition prior to any deductions.

Tuition	Mean	Median	Minimum	Maximum
Less than $5,000	$0.00	$0.00	$0.00	$0.00
$5,000 to $14,999	$100.00	$0.00	$0.00	$500.00
$15,000 or more	$2,042.50	$1,585.00	$0.00	$5,000.00

Table 57 What was the percentage change in the library's total budget for special collections for the 2013-14 academic year?

Table 57.1.1 What was the percentage change in the library's total budget for special collections for the 2013-14 academic year?

	Mean	Median	Minimum	Maximum
Entire sample	0.71%	0.00%	-90.00%	100.00%

Table 57.1.2 What was the percentage change in the library's total budget for special collections for the 2013-14 academic year? Broken out by type of college.

Type of College	Mean	Median	Minimum	Maximum
Community college	14.29%	0.00%	0.00%	100.00%
4-year BA- or MA-granting college	0.00%	0.00%	0.00%	0.00%
PhD-granting college or research university	-45.00%	-45.00%	-90.00%	0.00%

Table 57.1.3 What was the percentage change in the library's total budget for special collections for the 2013-14 academic year? Broken out by full-time equivalent enrollment of the college.

Enrollment	Mean	Median	Minimum	Maximum
Less than 2,500	0.00%	0.00%	0.00%	0.00%
2,500 to 7,499	25.00%	0.00%	0.00%	100.00%
7,500 or more	-30.00%	0.00%	-90.00%	0.00%

Table 57.1.4 What was the percentage change in the library's total budget for special collections for the 2013-14 academic year? Broken out by public or private status of the college.

Public or Private	Mean	Median	Minimum	Maximum
Public	0.91%	0.00%	-90.00%	100.00%
Private	0.00%	0.00%	0.00%	0.00%

Table 57.1.5 What was the percentage change in the library's total budget for special collections for the 2013-14 academic year? Broken out by annual full-time tuition prior to any deductions.

Tuition	Mean	Median	Minimum	Maximum
Less than $5,000	0.00%	0.00%	0.00%	0.00%
$5,000 to $14,999	25.00%	0.00%	0.00%	100.00%
$15,000 or more	-22.50%	0.00%	-90.00%	0.00%

Table 58 What is the expected percentage change in the library's total budget for special collections for the 2014-15 academic year?

Table 58.1.1 What is the expected percentage change in the library's total budget for special collections for the 2014-15 academic year?

	Mean	Median	Minimum	Maximum
Entire sample	0.00%	0.00%	0.00%	0.00%

Table 59 How would you describe the digitization efforts of your special collections division?

Table 59.1.1 How would you describe the digitization efforts of your special collections division?

	We don't have special collections	Have not digitized much	Have digitized small-scale projects	Have made a significant effort to digitize
Entire sample	20.83%	29.17%	41.67%	8.33%

Table 59.1.2 How would you describe the digitization efforts of your special collections division? Broken out by type of college.

Type of College	We don't have special collections	Have not digitized much	Have digitized small-scale projects	Have made a significant effort to digitize
Community college	36.36%	36.36%	18.18%	9.09%
4-year BA- or MA-granting college	0.00%	16.67%	83.33%	0.00%
PhD-granting college or research university	14.29%	28.57%	42.86%	14.29%

Table 59.1.3 How would you describe the digitization efforts of your special collections division? Broken out by full-time equivalent enrollment of the college.

Enrollment	We don't have special collections	Have not digitized much	Have digitized small-scale projects	Have made a significant effort to digitize
Less than 2,500	12.50%	37.50%	50.00%	0.00%
2,500 to 7,499	33.33%	33.33%	33.33%	0.00%
7,500 or more	14.29%	14.29%	42.86%	28.57%

Table 59.1.4 How would you describe the digitization efforts of your special collections division? Broken out by public or private status of the college.

Public or Private	We don't have special collections	Have not digitized much	Have digitized small-scale projects	Have made a significant effort to digitize
Public	26.32%	31.58%	31.58%	10.53%
Private	0.00%	20.00%	80.00%	0.00%

Table 59.1.5 How would you describe the digitization efforts of your special collections division? Broken out by annual full-time tuition prior to any deductions.

Tuition	We don't have special collections	Have not digitized much	Have digitized small-scale projects	Have made a significant effort to digitize
Less than $5,000	30.00%	50.00%	10.00%	10.00%
$5,000 to $14,999	28.57%	14.29%	57.14%	0.00%
$15,000 or more	0.00%	14.29%	71.43%	14.29%

Table 60 How would you characterize the library's attitude concerning the future of digitization of special collections at the library?

Table 60.1.1 How would you characterize the library's attitude concerning the future of digitization of special collections at the library?

	No Answer	Won't be doing much of this in the future	Definitely in the plans, but we are just getting started	Plans have been approved for significant investments	Plan on making a major push to digitize appropriate segments
Entire sample	4.17%	20.83%	75.00%	0.00%	0.00%

Table 60.1.2 How would you characterize the library's attitude concerning the future of digitization of special collections at the library? Broken out by type of college.

Type of College	No Answer	Won't be doing much of this in the future	Definitely in the plans, but we are just getting started	Plans have been approved for significant investments	Plan on making a major push to digitize appropriate segments
Community college	9.09%	27.27%	63.64%	0.00%	0.00%
4-year BA- or MA-granting college	0.00%	0.00%	100.00%	0.00%	0.00%
PhD-granting college or research university	0.00%	28.57%	71.43%	0.00%	0.00%

Table 60.1.3 How would you characterize the library's attitude concerning the future of digitization of special collections at the library? Broken out by full-time equivalent enrollment of the college.

Enrollment	No Answer	Won't be doing much of this in the future	Definitely in the plans, but we are just getting started	Plans have been approved for significant investments	Plan on making a major push to digitize appropriate segments
Less than 2,500	0.00%	12.50%	87.50%	0.00%	0.00%
2,500 to 7,499	11.11%	11.11%	77.78%	0.00%	0.00%
7,500 or more	0.00%	42.86%	57.14%	0.00%	0.00%

Table 60.1.4 How would you characterize the library's attitude concerning the future of digitization of special collections at the library? Broken out by public or private status of the college.

Public or Private	No Answer	Won't be doing much of this in the future	Definitely in the plans, but we are just getting started	Plans have been approved for significant investments	Plan on making a major push to digitize appropriate segments
Public	5.26%	21.05%	73.68%	0.00%	0.00%
Private	0.00%	20.00%	80.00%	0.00%	0.00%

Table 60.1.5 How would you characterize the library's attitude concerning the future of digitization of special collections at the library? Broken out by annual full-time tuition prior to any deductions.

Tuition	No Answer	Won't be doing much of this in the future	Definitely in the plans, but we are just getting started	Plans have been approved for significant investments	Plan on making a major push to digitize appropriate segments
Less than $5,000	10.00%	20.00%	70.00%	0.00%	0.00%
$5,000 to $14,999	0.00%	28.57%	71.43%	0.00%	0.00%
$15,000 or more	0.00%	14.29%	85.71%	0.00%	0.00%

Chapter 11 – Spending Trends

Table 61 What are the library's spending plans for video streaming in the next year?

Table 61.1.1 What are the library's spending plans for video streaming in the next year?

	Decrease substantially	Decrease	Remain the same	Increase	Increase substantially	No current or planned spending
Entire sample	0.00%	4.17%	33.33%	16.67%	4.17%	41.67%

Table 61.1.2 What are the library's spending plans for video streaming in the next year? Broken out by type of college.

Type of College	Decrease substantially	Decrease	Remain the same	Increase	Increase substantially	No current or planned spending
Community college	0.00%	9.09%	45.45%	27.27%	9.09%	9.09%
4-year BA- or MA- granting college	0.00%	0.00%	50.00%	0.00%	0.00%	50.00%
PhD-granting college or research university	0.00%	0.00%	0.00%	14.29%	0.00%	85.71%

Table 61.1.3 What are the library's spending plans for video streaming in the next year? Broken out by full-time equivalent enrollment of the college.

Enrollment	Decrease substantially	Decrease	Remain the same	Increase	Increase substantially	No current or planned spending
Less than 2,500	0.00%	12.50%	37.50%	0.00%	12.50%	37.50%
2,500 to 7,499	0.00%	0.00%	33.33%	22.22%	0.00%	44.44%
7,500 or more	0.00%	0.00%	28.57%	28.57%	0.00%	42.86%

Table 61.1.4 What are the library's spending plans for video streaming in the next year? Broken out by public or private status of the college.

Public or Private	Decrease substantially	Decrease	Remain the same	Increase	Increase substantially	No current or planned spending
Public	0.00%	5.26%	31.58%	21.05%	5.26%	36.84%
Private	0.00%	0.00%	40.00%	0.00%	0.00%	60.00%

Table 61.1.5 What are the library's spending plans for video streaming in the next year? Broken out by annual full-time tuition prior to any deductions.

Tuition	Decrease substantially	Decrease	Remain the same	Increase	Increase substantially	No current or planned spending
Less than $5,000	0.00%	10.00%	40.00%	20.00%	10.00%	20.00%
$5,000 to $14,999	0.00%	0.00%	28.57%	14.29%	0.00%	57.14%
$15,000 or more	0.00%	0.00%	28.57%	14.29%	0.00%	57.14%

Table 62 What are the library's spending plans for digital repository software and services in the next year?

Table 62.1.1 What are the library's spending plans for digital repository software and services in the next year?

	Decrease substantially	Decrease	Remain the same	Increase	Increase substantially	No current or planned spending
Entire sample	4.17%	8.33%	20.83%	20.83%	4.17%	41.67%

Table 62.1.2 What are the library's spending plans for digital repository software and services in the next year? Broken out by type of college.

Type of College	Decrease substantially	Decrease	Remain the same	Increase	Increase substantially	No current or planned spending
Community college	9.09%	9.09%	18.18%	9.09%	0.00%	54.55%
4-year BA- or MA- granting college	0.00%	16.67%	33.33%	16.67%	0.00%	33.33%
PhD- granting college or research university	0.00%	0.00%	14.29%	42.86%	14.29%	28.57%

Table 62.1.3 What are the library's spending plans for digital repository software and services in the next year? Broken out by full-time equivalent enrollment of the college.

Enrollment	Decrease substantially	Decrease	Remain the same	Increase	Increase substantially	No current or planned spending
Less than 2,500	0.00%	12.50%	12.50%	0.00%	0.00%	75.00%
2,500 to 7,499	11.11%	11.11%	22.22%	22.22%	11.11%	22.22%
7,500 or more	0.00%	0.00%	28.57%	42.86%	0.00%	28.57%

Table 62.1.4 What are the library's spending plans for digital repository software and services in the next year? Broken out by public or private status of the college.

Public or Private	Decrease substantially	Decrease	Remain the same	Increase	Increase substantially	No current or planned spending
Public	5.26%	10.53%	21.05%	26.32%	0.00%	36.84%
Private	0.00%	0.00%	20.00%	0.00%	20.00%	60.00%

Table 62.1.5 What are the library's spending plans for digital repository software and services in the next year? Broken out by annual full-time tuition prior to any deductions.

Tuition	Decrease substantially	Decrease	Remain the same	Increase	Increase substantially	No current or planned spending
Less than $5,000	0.00%	10.00%	20.00%	10.00%	0.00%	60.00%
$5,000 to $14,999	14.29%	14.29%	28.57%	28.57%	0.00%	14.29%
$15,000 or more	0.00%	0.00%	14.29%	28.57%	14.29%	42.86%

Table 63 What are the library's spending plans for cloud computing web storage devices in the next year?

Table 63.1.1 What are the library's spending plans for cloud computing web storage devices in the next year?

	Decrease substantially	Decrease	Remain the same	Increase	Increase substantially	No current or planned spending
Entire sample	0.00%	4.17%	16.67%	25.00%	0.00%	54.17%

Table 63.1.2 What are the library's spending plans for cloud computing web storage devices in the next year? Broken out by type of college.

Type of College	Decrease substantially	Decrease	Remain the same	Increase	Increase substantially	No current or planned spending
Community college	0.00%	9.09%	18.18%	9.09%	0.00%	63.64%
4-year BA- or MA- granting college	0.00%	0.00%	16.67%	33.33%	0.00%	50.00%
PhD- granting college or research university	0.00%	0.00%	14.29%	42.86%	0.00%	42.86%

Table 63.1.3 What are the library's spending plans for cloud computing web storage devices in the next year? Broken out by full-time equivalent enrollment of the college.

Enrollment	Decrease substantially	Decrease	Remain the same	Increase	Increase substantially	No current or planned spending
Less than 2,500	0.00%	12.50%	0.00%	12.50%	0.00%	75.00%
2,500 to 7,499	0.00%	0.00%	33.33%	22.22%	0.00%	44.44%
7,500 or more	0.00%	0.00%	14.29%	42.86%	0.00%	42.86%

Table 63.1.4 What are the library's spending plans for cloud computing web storage devices in the next year? Broken out by public or private status of the college.

Public or Private	Decrease substantially	Decrease	Remain the same	Increase	Increase substantially	No current or planned spending
Public	0.00%	5.26%	21.05%	21.05%	0.00%	52.63%
Private	0.00%	0.00%	0.00%	40.00%	0.00%	60.00%

Table 63.1.5 What are the library's spending plans for cloud computing web storage devices in the next year? Broken out by annual full-time tuition prior to any deductions.

Tuition	Decrease substantially	Decrease	Remain the same	Increase	Increase substantially	No current or planned spending
Less than $5,000	0.00%	10.00%	20.00%	10.00%	0.00%	60.00%
$5,000 to $14,999	0.00%	0.00%	28.57%	14.29%	0.00%	57.14%
$15,000 or more	0.00%	0.00%	0.00%	57.14%	0.00%	42.86%

Table 64 What are the library's spending plans for RFID, barcoding, and other inventory-tracking technologies in the next year?

Table 64.1.1 What are the library's spending plans for RFID, barcoding, and other inventory-tracking technologies in the next year?

	No Answer	Decrease substantially	Decrease	Remain the same	Increase	Increase substantially	No current or planned spending
Entire sample	4.17%	4.17%	8.33%	37.50%	0.00%	0.00%	45.83%

Table 64.1.2 What are the library's spending plans for RFID, barcoding, and other inventory-tracking technologies in the next year? Broken out by type of college.

Type of College	No Answer	Decrease substantially	Decrease	Remain the same	Increase	Increase substantially	No current or planned spending
Community college	0.00%	9.09%	0.00%	45.45%	0.00%	0.00%	45.45%
4-year BA- or MA-granting college	16.67%	0.00%	16.67%	16.67%	0.00%	0.00%	50.00%
PhD-granting college or research university	0.00%	0.00%	14.29%	42.86%	0.00%	0.00%	42.86%

Table 64.1.3 What are the library's spending plans for RFID, barcoding, and other inventory-tracking technologies in the next year? Broken out by full-time equivalent enrollment of the college.

Enrollment	No Answer	Decrease substantially	Decrease	Remain the same	Increase	Increase substantially	No current or planned spending
Less than 2,500	12.50%	12.50%	12.50%	25.00%	0.00%	0.00%	37.50%
2,500 to 7,499	0.00%	0.00%	11.11%	44.44%	0.00%	0.00%	44.44%
7,500 or more	0.00%	0.00%	0.00%	42.86%	0.00%	0.00%	57.14%

Table 64.1.4 What are the library's spending plans for RFID, barcoding, and other inventory-tracking technologies in the next year? Broken out by public or private status of the college.

Public or Private	No Answer	Decrease substantially	Decrease	Remain the same	Increase	Increase substantially	No current or planned spending
Public	0.00%	5.26%	0.00%	47.37%	0.00%	0.00%	47.37%
Private	20.00%	0.00%	40.00%	0.00%	0.00%	0.00%	40.00%

Table 64.1.5 What are the library's spending plans for RFID, barcoding, and other inventory-tracking technologies in the next year? Broken out by annual full-time tuition prior to any deductions.

Tuition	No Answer	Decrease substantially	Decrease	Remain the same	Increase	Increase substantially	No current or planned spending
Less than $5,000	0.00%	10.00%	0.00%	40.00%	0.00%	0.00%	50.00%
$5,000 to $14,999	0.00%	0.00%	0.00%	71.43%	0.00%	0.00%	28.57%
$15,000 or more	14.29%	0.00%	28.57%	0.00%	0.00%	0.00%	57.14%

Table 65 What are the library's spending plans for book- or serials-binding technology and services in the next year?

Table 65.1.1 What are the library's spending plans for book- or serials-binding technology and services in the next year?

	No Answer	Decrease substantially	Decrease	Remain the same	Increase	Increase substantially	No current or planneds pending
Entire sample	4.17%	25.00%	25.00%	29.17%	0.00%	0.00%	16.67%

Table 65.1.2 What are the library's spending plans for book- or serials-binding technology and services in the next year? Broken out by type of college.

Type of College	No Answer	Decrease substantially	Decrease	Remain the same	Increase	Increase substantially	No current or planned spending
Community college	9.09%	18.18%	27.27%	18.18%	0.00%	0.00%	27.27%
4-year BA- or MA-granting college	0.00%	66.67%	0.00%	33.33%	0.00%	0.00%	0.00%
PhD-granting college or research university	0.00%	0.00%	42.86%	42.86%	0.00%	0.00%	14.29%

Table 65.1.3 What are the library's spending plans for book- or serials-binding technology and services in the next year? Broken out by full-time equivalent enrollment of the college.

Enrollment	No Answer	Decrease substantially	Decrease	Remain the same	Increase	Increase substantially	No current or planned spending
Less than 2,500	0.00%	25.00%	0.00%	37.50%	0.00%	0.00%	37.50%
2,500 to 7,499	11.11%	22.22%	44.44%	11.11%	0.00%	0.00%	11.11%
7,500 or more	0.00%	28.57%	28.57%	42.86%	0.00%	0.00%	0.00%

Table 65.1.4 What are the library's spending plans for book- or serials-binding technology and services in the next year? Broken out by public or private status of the college.

Public or Private	No Answer	Decrease substantially	Decrease	Remain the same	Increase	Increase substantially	No current or planned spending
Public	5.26%	26.32%	26.32%	21.05%	0.00%	0.00%	21.05%
Private	0.00%	20.00%	20.00%	60.00%	0.00%	0.00%	0.00%

Table 65.1.5 What are the library's spending plans for book- or serials-binding technology and services in the next year? Broken out by annual full-time tuition prior to any deductions.

Tuition	No Answer	Decrease substantially	Decrease	Remain the same	Increase	Increase substantially	No current or planned spending
Less than $5,000	10.00%	30.00%	20.00%	20.00%	0.00%	0.00%	20.00%
$5,000 to $14,999	0.00%	28.57%	14.29%	28.57%	0.00%	0.00%	28.57%
$15,000 or more	0.00%	14.29%	42.86%	42.86%	0.00%	0.00%	0.00%

Table 66 What are the library's spending plans for artwork for the library in the next year?

Table 66.1.1 What are the library's spending plans for artwork for the library in the next year?

	Decrease substantially	Decrease	Remain the same	Increase	Increase substantially	No current or planned spending
Entire sample	12.50%	4.17%	20.83%	20.83%	0.00%	41.67%

Table 66.1.2 What are the library's spending plans for artwork for the library in the next year? Broken out by type of college.

Type of College	Decrease substantially	Decrease	Remain the same	Increase	Increase substantially	No current or planned spending
Community college	18.18%	0.00%	18.18%	18.18%	0.00%	45.45%
4-year BA- or MA- granting college	16.67%	0.00%	16.67%	33.33%	0.00%	33.33%
PhD- granting college or research university	0.00%	14.29%	28.57%	14.29%	0.00%	42.86%

Table 66.1.3 What are the library's spending plans for artwork for the library in the next year? Broken out by full-time equivalent enrollment of the college.

Enrollment	Decrease substantially	Decrease	Remain the same	Increase	Increase substantially	No current or planned spending
Less than 2,500	25.00%	0.00%	0.00%	12.50%	0.00%	62.50%
2,500 to 7,499	11.11%	11.11%	33.33%	11.11%	0.00%	33.33%
7,500 or more	0.00%	0.00%	28.57%	42.86%	0.00%	28.57%

Table 66.1.4 What are the library's spending plans for artwork for the library in the next year? Broken out by public or private status of the college.

Public or Private	Decrease substantially	Decrease	Remain the same	Increase	Increase substantially	No current or planned spending
Public	10.53%	0.00%	26.32%	21.05%	0.00%	42.11%
Private	20.00%	20.00%	0.00%	20.00%	0.00%	40.00%

Table 66.1.5 What are the library's spending plans for artwork for the library in the next year? Broken out by annual full-time tuition prior to any deductions.

Tuition	Decrease substantially	Decrease	Remain the same	Increase	Increase substantially	No current or planned spending
Less than $5,000	20.00%	0.00%	20.00%	20.00%	0.00%	40.00%
$5,000 to $14,999	0.00%	0.00%	28.57%	28.57%	0.00%	42.86%
$15,000 or more	14.29%	14.29%	14.29%	14.29%	0.00%	42.86%

Table 67 What are the library's spending plans for whiteboards, classroom clickers, and other presentation/testing technologies in the next year?

Table 67.1.1 What are the library's spending plans for whiteboards, classroom clickers, and other presentation/testing technologies in the next year?

	Decrease substantially	Decrease	Remain the same	Increase	Increase substantially	No current or planned spending
Entire sample	8.33%	4.17%	29.17%	12.50%	0.00%	45.83%

Table 67.1.2 What are the library's spending plans for whiteboards, classroom clickers, and other presentation/testing technologies in the next year? Broken out by type of college.

Type of College	Decrease substantially	Decrease	Remain the same	Increase	Increase substantially	No current or planned spending
Community college	9.09%	9.09%	18.18%	9.09%	0.00%	54.55%
4-year BA- or MA- granting college	0.00%	0.00%	50.00%	16.67%	0.00%	33.33%
PhD- granting college or research university	14.29%	0.00%	28.57%	14.29%	0.00%	42.86%

Table 67.1.3 What are the library's spending plans for whiteboards, classroom clickers, and other presentation/testing technologies in the next year? Broken out by full-time equivalent enrollment of the college.

Enrollment	Decrease substantially	Decrease	Remain the same	Increase	Increase substantially	No current or planned spending
Less than 2,500	12.50%	12.50%	12.50%	0.00%	0.00%	62.50%
2,500 to 7,499	11.11%	0.00%	44.44%	0.00%	0.00%	44.44%
7,500 or more	0.00%	0.00%	28.57%	42.86%	0.00%	28.57%

Table 67.1.4 What are the library's spending plans for whiteboards, classroom clickers, and other presentation/testing technologies in the next year? Broken out by public or private status of the college.

Public or Private	Decrease substantially	Decrease	Remain the same	Increase	Increase substantially	No current or planned spending
Public	5.26%	5.26%	31.58%	10.53%	0.00%	47.37%
Private	20.00%	0.00%	20.00%	20.00%	0.00%	40.00%

Table 67.1.5 What are the library's spending plans for whiteboards, classroom clickers, and other presentation/testing technologies in the next year? Broken out by annual full-time tuition prior to any deductions.

Tuition	Decrease substantially	Decrease	Remain the same	Increase	Increase substantially	No current or planned spending
Less than $5,000	0.00%	10.00%	20.00%	10.00%	0.00%	60.00%
$5,000 to $14,999	14.29%	0.00%	42.86%	14.29%	0.00%	28.57%
$15,000 or more	14.29%	0.00%	28.57%	14.29%	0.00%	42.86%

Table 68 What are the library's spending plans for mobile computing and telecommunications devices in the next year?

Table 68.1.1 What are the library's spending plans for mobile computing and telecommunications devices in the next year?

	Decrease substantially	Decrease	Remain the same	Increase	Increase substantially	No current or planned spending
Entire sample	0.00%	4.17%	16.67%	37.50%	4.17%	37.50%

Table 68.1.2 What are the library's spending plans for mobile computing and telecommunications devices in the next year? Broken out by type of college.

Type of College	Decrease substantially	Decrease	Remain the same	Increase	Increase substantially	No current or planned spending
Community college	0.00%	9.09%	9.09%	36.36%	0.00%	45.45%
4-year BA- or MA- granting college	0.00%	0.00%	16.67%	33.33%	16.67%	33.33%
PhD- granting college or research university	0.00%	0.00%	28.57%	42.86%	0.00%	28.57%

Table 68.1.3 What are the library's spending plans for mobile computing and telecommunications devices in the next year? Broken out by full-time equivalent enrollment of the college.

Enrollment	Decrease substantially	Decrease	Remain the same	Increase	Increase substantially	No current or planned spending
Less than 2,500	0.00%	12.50%	12.50%	37.50%	0.00%	37.50%
2,500 to 7,499	0.00%	0.00%	33.33%	11.11%	11.11%	44.44%
7,500 or more	0.00%	0.00%	0.00%	71.43%	0.00%	28.57%

Table 68.1.4 What are the library's spending plans for mobile computing and telecommunications devices in the next year? Broken out by public or private status of the college.

Public or Private	Decrease substantially	Decrease	Remain the same	Increase	Increase substantially	No current or planned spending
Public	0.00%	5.26%	15.79%	36.84%	5.26%	36.84%
Private	0.00%	0.00%	20.00%	40.00%	0.00%	40.00%

Table 68.1.5 What are the library's spending plans for mobile computing and telecommunications devices in the next year? Broken out by annual full-time tuition prior to any deductions.

Tuition	Decrease substantially	Decrease	Remain the same	Increase	Increase substantially	No current or planned spending
Less than $5,000	0.00%	10.00%	30.00%	40.00%	0.00%	20.00%
$5,000 to $14,999	0.00%	0.00%	0.00%	28.57%	14.29%	57.14%
$15,000 or more	0.00%	0.00%	14.29%	42.86%	0.00%	42.86%

Table 69 What are the library's spending plans for public relations or marketing services for the library in the next year?

Table 69.1.1 What are the library's spending plans for public relations or marketing services for the library in the next year?

	Decrease substantially	Decrease	Remain the same	Increase	Increase substantially	No current or planned spending
Entire sample	0.00%	8.33%	33.33%	29.17%	4.17%	25.00%

Table 69.1.2 What are the library's spending plans for public relations or marketing services for the library in the next year? Broken out by type of college.

Type of College	Decrease substantially	Decrease	Remain the same	Increase	Increase substantially	No current or planned spending
Community college	0.00%	0.00%	45.45%	9.09%	9.09%	36.36%
4-year BA- or MA- granting college	0.00%	16.67%	16.67%	66.67%	0.00%	0.00%
PhD- granting college or research university	0.00%	14.29%	28.57%	28.57%	0.00%	28.57%

Table 69.1.3 What are the library's spending plans for public relations or marketing services for the library in the next year? Broken out by full-time equivalent enrollment of the college.

Enrollment	Decrease substantially	Decrease	Remain the same	Increase	Increase substantially	No current or planned spending
Less than 2,500	0.00%	12.50%	25.00%	12.50%	12.50%	37.50%
2,500 to 7,499	0.00%	11.11%	44.44%	33.33%	0.00%	11.11%
7,500 or more	0.00%	0.00%	28.57%	42.86%	0.00%	28.57%

Table 69.1.4 What are the library's spending plans for public relations or marketing services for the library in the next year? Broken out by public or private status of the college.

Public or Private	Decrease substantially	Decrease	Remain the same	Increase	Increase substantially	No current or planned spending
Public	0.00%	5.26%	31.58%	31.58%	5.26%	26.32%
Private	0.00%	20.00%	40.00%	20.00%	0.00%	20.00%

Table 69.1.5 What are the library's spending plans for public relations or marketing services for the library in the next year? Broken out by annual full-time tuition prior to any deductions.

Tuition	Decrease substantially	Decrease	Remain the same	Increase	Increase substantially	No current or planned spending
Less than $5,000	0.00%	0.00%	30.00%	20.00%	10.00%	40.00%
$5,000 to $14,999	0.00%	14.29%	28.57%	42.86%	0.00%	14.29%
$15,000 or more	0.00%	14.29%	42.86%	28.57%	0.00%	14.29%

Table 70 What are the library's spending plans for applications software for media and computer centers or information commons in the next year?

Table 70.1.1 What are the library's spending plans for applications software for media and computer centers or information commons in the next year?

	Decrease substantially	Decrease	Remain the same	Increase	Increase substantially	No current or planned spending
Entire sample	0.00%	4.17%	41.67%	8.33%	4.17%	41.67%

Table 70.1.2 What are the library's spending plans for applications software for media and computer centers or information commons in the next year? Broken out by type of college.

Type of College	Decrease substantially	Decrease	Remain the same	Increase	Increase substantially	No current or planned spending
Community college	0.00%	9.09%	45.45%	0.00%	0.00%	45.45%
4-year BA- or MA- granting college	0.00%	0.00%	50.00%	0.00%	16.67%	33.33%
PhD- granting college or research university	0.00%	0.00%	28.57%	28.57%	0.00%	42.86%

Table 70.1.3 What are the library's spending plans for applications software for media and computer centers or information commons in the next year? Broken out by full-time equivalent enrollment of the college.

Enrollment	Decrease substantially	Decrease	Remain the same	Increase	Increase substantially	No current or planned spending
Less than 2,500	0.00%	12.50%	37.50%	0.00%	0.00%	50.00%
2,500 to 7,499	0.00%	0.00%	55.56%	0.00%	11.11%	33.33%
7,500 or more	0.00%	0.00%	28.57%	28.57%	0.00%	42.86%

Table 70.1.4 What are the library's spending plans for applications software for media and computer centers or information commons in the next year? Broken out by public or private status of the college.

Public or Private	Decrease substantially	Decrease	Remain the same	Increase	Increase substantially	No current or planned spending
Public	0.00%	5.26%	42.11%	10.53%	5.26%	36.84%
Private	0.00%	0.00%	40.00%	0.00%	0.00%	60.00%

Table 70.1.5 What are the library's spending plans for applications software for media and computer centers or information commons in the next year? Broken out by annual full-time tuition prior to any deductions.

Tuition	Decrease substantially	Decrease	Remain the same	Increase	Increase substantially	No current or planned spending
Less than $5,000	0.00%	10.00%	60.00%	0.00%	0.00%	30.00%
$5,000 to $14,999	0.00%	0.00%	28.57%	14.29%	14.29%	42.86%
$15,000 or more	0.00%	0.00%	28.57%	14.29%	0.00%	57.14%

Table 71 What are the library's spending plans for librarian travel and conferences in the next year?

Table 71.1.1 What are the library's spending plans for librarian travel and conferences in the next year?

	Decrease substantially	Decrease	Remain the same	Increase	Increase substantially	No current or planned spending
Entire sample	8.33%	12.50%	66.67%	8.33%	0.00%	4.17%

Table 71.1.2 What are the library's spending plans for librarian travel and conferences in the next year? Broken out by type of college.

Type of College	Decrease substantially	Decrease	Remain the same	Increase	Increase substantially	No current or planned spending
Community college	18.18%	18.18%	54.55%	0.00%	0.00%	9.09%
4-year BA- or MA- granting college	0.00%	0.00%	66.67%	33.33%	0.00%	0.00%
PhD- granting college or research university	0.00%	14.29%	85.71%	0.00%	0.00%	0.00%

Table 71.1.3 What are the library's spending plans for librarian travel and conferences in the next year? Broken out by full-time equivalent enrollment of the college.

Enrollment	Decrease substantially	Decrease	Remain the same	Increase	Increase substantially	No current or planned spending
Less than 2,500	25.00%	0.00%	50.00%	12.50%	0.00%	12.50%
2,500 to 7,499	0.00%	11.11%	77.78%	11.11%	0.00%	0.00%
7,500 or more	0.00%	28.57%	71.43%	0.00%	0.00%	0.00%

Table 71.1.4 What are the library's spending plans for librarian travel and conferences in the next year? Broken out by public or private status of the college.

Public or Private	Decrease substantially	Decrease	Remain the same	Increase	Increase substantially	No current or planned spending
Public	10.53%	10.53%	68.42%	5.26%	0.00%	5.26%
Private	0.00%	20.00%	60.00%	20.00%	0.00%	0.00%

Table 71.1.5 What are the library's spending plans for librarian travel and conferences in the next year? Broken out by annual full-time tuition prior to any deductions.

Tuition	Decrease substantially	Decrease	Remain the same	Increase	Increase substantially	No current or planned spending
Less than $5,000	10.00%	20.00%	50.00%	10.00%	0.00%	10.00%
$5,000 to $14,999	14.29%	0.00%	85.71%	0.00%	0.00%	0.00%
$15,000 or more	0.00%	14.29%	71.43%	14.29%	0.00%	0.00%

Table 72 What are the library's spending plans for librarian staff training in the next year?

Table 72.1.1 What are the library's spending plans for librarian staff training in the next year?

	Decrease substantially	Decrease	Remain the same	Increase	Increase substantially	No current or planned spending
Entire sample	4.17%	8.33%	70.83%	12.50%	0.00%	4.17%

Table 72.1.2 What are the library's spending plans for librarian staff training in the next year? Broken out by type of college.

Type of College	Decrease substantially	Decrease	Remain the same	Increase	Increase substantially	No current or planned spending
Community college	9.09%	9.09%	63.64%	9.09%	0.00%	9.09%
4-year BA- or MA-granting college	0.00%	0.00%	66.67%	33.33%	0.00%	0.00%
PhD-granting college or research university	0.00%	14.29%	85.71%	0.00%	0.00%	0.00%

Table 72.1.3 What are the library's spending plans for librarian staff training in the next year? Broken out by full-time equivalent enrollment of the college.

Enrollment	Decrease substantially	Decrease	Remain the same	Increase	Increase substantially	No current or planned spending
Less than 2,500	12.50%	12.50%	50.00%	25.00%	0.00%	0.00%
2,500 to 7,499	0.00%	0.00%	77.78%	11.11%	0.00%	11.11%
7,500 or more	0.00%	14.29%	85.71%	0.00%	0.00%	0.00%

Table 72.1.4 What are the library's spending plans for librarian staff training in the next year? Broken out by public or private status of the college.

Public or Private	Decrease substantially	Decrease	Remain the same	Increase	Increase substantially	No current or planned spending
Public	5.26%	5.26%	73.68%	10.53%	0.00%	5.26%
Private	0.00%	20.00%	60.00%	20.00%	0.00%	0.00%

Table 72.1.5 What are the library's spending plans for librarian staff training in the next year? Broken out by annual full-time tuition prior to any deductions.

Tuition	Decrease substantially	Decrease	Remain the same	Increase	Increase substantially	No current or planned spending
Less than $5,000	0.00%	10.00%	60.00%	20.00%	0.00%	10.00%
$5,000 to $14,999	14.29%	0.00%	85.71%	0.00%	0.00%	0.00%
$15,000 or more	0.00%	14.29%	71.43%	14.29%	0.00%	0.00%

Chapter 12 – Computing Devices and Library Information Technology

Table 73 Does the library lend laptop computers to library patrons?

Table 73.1.1 Does the library lend laptop computers to library patrons?

	No Answer	Yes	No
Entire sample	0.00%	45.83%	54.17%

Table 73.1.2 Does the library lend laptop computers to library patrons? Broken out by type of college.

Type of College	Yes	No
Community college	36.36%	63.64%
4-year BA- or MA-granting college	66.67%	33.33%
PhD-granting college or research university	42.86%	57.14%

Table 73.1.3 Does the library lend laptop computers to library patrons? Broken out by full-time equivalent enrollment of the college.

Enrollment	Yes	No
Less than 2,500	62.50%	37.50%
2,500 to 7,499	22.22%	77.78%
7,500 or more	57.14%	42.86%

Table 73.1.4 Does the library lend laptop computers to library patrons? Broken out by public or private status of the college.

Public or Private	Yes	No
Public	47.37%	52.63%
Private	40.00%	60.00%

Table 73.1.5 Does the library lend laptop computers to library patrons? Broken out by annual full-time tuition prior to any deductions.

Tuition	Yes	No
Less than $5,000	40.00%	60.00%
$5,000 to $14,999	57.14%	42.86%
$15,000 or more	42.86%	57.14%

Table 74 Does the library lend tablet computers to library patrons?

Table 74.1.1 Does the library lend tablet computers to library patrons?

	No Answer	Yes	No
Entire sample	0.00%	16.67%	83.33%

Table 74.1.2 Does the library lend tablet computers to library patrons? Broken out by type of college.

Type of College	Yes	No
Community college	9.09%	90.91%
4-year BA- or MA-granting college	33.33%	66.67%
PhD-granting college or research university	14.29%	85.71%

Table 74.1.3 Does the library lend tablet computers to library patrons? Broken out by full-time equivalent enrollment of the college.

Enrollment	Yes	No
Less than 2,500	0.00%	100.00%
2,500 to 7,499	33.33%	66.67%
7,500 or more	14.29%	85.71%

Table 74.1.4 Does the library lend tablet computers to library patrons? Broken out by public or private status of the college.

Public or Private	Yes	No
Public	21.05%	78.95%
Private	0.00%	100.00%

Table 74.1.5 Does the library lend tablet computers to library patrons? Broken out by annual full-time tuition prior to any deductions.

Tuition	Yes	No
Less than $5,000	10.00%	90.00%
$5,000 to $14,999	42.86%	57.14%
$15,000 or more	0.00%	100.00%

Table 75 Does the library lend e-book reading devices to library patrons?

Table 75.1.1 Does the library lend e-book reading devices to library patrons?

	No Answer	Yes	No
Entire sample	0.00%	29.17%	70.83%

Table 75.1.2 Does the library lend e-book reading devices to library patrons? Broken out by type of college.

Type of College	Yes	No
Community college	27.27%	72.73%
4-year BA- or MA-granting college	33.33%	66.67%
PhD-granting college or research university	28.57%	71.43%

Table 75.1.3 Does the library lend e-book reading devices to library patrons? Broken out by full-time equivalent enrollment of the college.

Enrollment	Yes	No
Less than 2,500	25.00%	75.00%
2,500 to 7,499	33.33%	66.67%
7,500 or more	28.57%	71.43%

Table 75.1.4 Does the library lend e-book reading devices to library patrons? Broken out by public or private status of the college.

Public or Private	Yes	No
Public	31.58%	68.42%
Private	20.00%	80.00%

Table 75.1.5 Does the library lend e-book reading devices to library patrons? Broken out by annual full-time tuition prior to any deductions.

Tuition	Yes	No
Less than $5,000	20.00%	80.00%
$5,000 to $14,999	42.86%	57.14%
$15,000 or more	28.57%	71.43%

Table 76 If the library lends laptop computers to patrons, what is the total stock of devices available for loan?

Table 76.1.1 If the library lends laptop computers to patrons, what is the total stock of devices available for loan?

	Mean	Median	Minimum	Maximum
Entire sample	27.36	20.00	2.00	100.00

Table 76.1.2 If the library lends laptop computers to patrons, what is the total stock of devices available for loan? Broken out by type of college.

Type of College	Mean	Median	Minimum	Maximum
Community college	16.75	17.50	2.00	30.00
4-year BA- or MA-granting college	41.50	31.50	3.00	100.00
PhD-granting college or research university	22.67	26.00	2.00	40.00

Table 76.1.3 If the library lends laptop computers to patrons, what is the total stock of devices available for loan? Broken out by full-time equivalent enrollment of the college.

Enrollment	Mean	Median	Minimum	Maximum
Less than 2,500	9.00	3.00	2.00	20.00
2,500 to 7,499	42.50	42.50	40.00	45.00
7,500 or more	42.75	28.00	15.00	100.00

Table 76.1.4 If the library lends laptop computers to patrons, what is the total stock of devices available for loan? Broken out by public or private status of the college.

Public or Private	Mean	Median	Minimum	Maximum
Public	31.11	26.00	2.00	100.00
Private	10.50	10.50	3.00	18.00

Table 76.1.5 If the library lends laptop computers to patrons, what is the total stock of devices available for loan? Broken out by annual full-time tuition prior to any deductions.

Tuition	Mean	Median	Minimum	Maximum
Less than $5,000	16.75	17.50	2.00	30.00
$5,000 to $14,999	46.75	42.50	2.00	100.00
$15,000 or more	15.67	18.00	3.00	26.00

Table 77 If the library lends tablet computers to patrons, what is the total stock of devices available for loan?

Table 77.1.1 If the library lends tablet computers to patrons, what is the total stock of devices available for loan?

	Mean	Median	Minimum	Maximum
Entire sample	14.25	8.00	1.00	40.00

Table 77.1.2 If the library lends tablet computers to patrons, what is the total stock of devices available for loan? Broken out by type of college.

Type of College	Mean	Median	Minimum	Maximum
Community college	1.00	1.00	1.00	1.00
4-year BA- or MA-granting college	8.00	8.00	6.00	10.00
PhD-granting college or research university	40.00	40.00	40.00	40.00

Table 77.1.3 If the library lends tablet computers to patrons, what is the total stock of devices available for loan? Broken out by full-time equivalent enrollment of the college.

Enrollment	Mean	Median	Minimum	Maximum
Less than 2,500	N/A	N/A	N/A	N/A
2,500 to 7,499	17.00	10.00	1.00	40.00
7,500 or more	6.00	6.00	6.00	6.00

The Survey of Academic Libraries, 2014-15 Edition

Table 77.1.4 If the library lends tablet computers to patrons, what is the total stock of devices available for loan? Broken out by public or private status of the college.

Public or Private	Mean	Median	Minimum	Maximum
Public	14.25	8.00	1.00	40.00
Private	N/A	N/A	N/A	N/A

Table 77.1.5 If the library lends tablet computers to patrons, what is the total stock of devices available for loan? Broken out by annual full-time tuition prior to any deductions.

Tuition	Mean	Median	Minimum	Maximum
Less than $5,000	1.00	1.00	1.00	1.00
$5,000 to $14,999	18.67	10.00	6.00	40.00
$15,000 or more	N/A	N/A	N/A	N/A

Table 78 If the library lends e-book reading devices to patrons, what is the total stock of devices available for loan?

Table 78.1.1 If the library lends e-book reading devices to patrons, what is the total stock of devices available for loan?

	Mean	Median	Minimum	Maximum
Entire sample	7.71	3.00	1.00	30.00

Table 78.1.2 If the library lends e-book reading devices to patrons, what is the total stock of devices available for loan? Broken out by type of college.

Type of College	Mean	Median	Minimum	Maximum
Community college	4.67	3.00	1.00	10.00
4-year BA- or MA-granting college	3.50	3.50	2.00	5.00
PhD-granting college or research university	16.50	16.50	3.00	30.00

Table 78.1.3 If the library lends e-book reading devices to patrons, what is the total stock of devices available for loan? Broken out by full-time equivalent enrollment of the college.

Enrollment	Mean	Median	Minimum	Maximum
Less than 2,500	2.50	2.50	2.00	3.00
2,500 to 7,499	5.33	5.00	1.00	10.00
7,500 or more	16.50	16.50	3.00	30.00

Table 78.1.4 If the library lends e-book reading devices to patrons, what is the total stock of devices available for loan? Broken out by public or private status of the college.

Public or Private	Mean	Median	Minimum	Maximum
Public	8.67	4.00	1.00	30.00
Private	2.00	2.00	2.00	2.00

Table 78.1.5 If the library lends e-book reading devices to patrons, what is the total stock of devices available for loan? Broken out by annual full-time tuition prior to any deductions.

Tuition	Mean	Median	Minimum	Maximum
Less than $5,000	2.00	2.00	1.00	3.00
$5,000 to $14,999	15.00	10.00	5.00	30.00
$15,000 or more	2.50	2.50	2.00	3.00

Table 79 How much does the library plan to spend in the next year on laptop computers?

Table 79.1.1 How much does the library plan to spend in the next year on laptop computers?

	Mean	Median	Minimum	Maximum
Entire sample	$138.89	$0.00	$0.00	$2,500.00

Table 79.1.2 How much does the library plan to spend in the next year on laptop computers? Broken out by type of college.

Type of College	Mean	Median	Minimum	Maximum
Community college	$227.27	$0.00	$0.00	$2,500.00
4-year BA- or MA-granting college	$0.00	$0.00	$0.00	$0.00
PhD-granting college or research university	$0.00	$0.00	$0.00	$0.00

Table 79.1.3 How much does the library plan to spend in the next year on laptop computers? Broken out by full-time equivalent enrollment of the college.

Enrollment	Mean	Median	Minimum	Maximum
Less than 2,500	$0.00	$0.00	$0.00	$0.00
2,500 to 7,499	$357.14	$0.00	$0.00	$2,500.00
7,500 or more	$0.00	$0.00	$0.00	$0.00

The Survey of Academic Libraries, 2014-15 Edition

Table 79.1.4 How much does the library plan to spend in the next year on laptop computers? Broken out by public or private status of the college.

Public or Private	Mean	Median	Minimum	Maximum
Public	$166.67	$0.00	$0.00	$2,500.00
Private	$0.00	$0.00	$0.00	$0.00

Table 79.1.5 How much does the library plan to spend in the next year on laptop computers? Broken out by annual full-time tuition prior to any deductions.

Tuition	Mean	Median	Minimum	Maximum
Less than $5,000	$277.78	$0.00	$0.00	$2,500.00
$5,000 to $14,999	$0.00	$0.00	$0.00	$0.00
$15,000 or more	$0.00	$0.00	$0.00	$0.00

Table 80 How much does the library plan to spend in the next year on tablet computers?

Table 80.1.1 How much does the library plan to spend in the next year on tablet computers?

	Mean	Median	Minimum	Maximum
Entire sample	$555.56	$0.00	$0.00	$5,000.00

Table 80.1.2 How much does the library plan to spend in the next year on tablet computers? Broken out by type of college.

Type of College	Mean	Median	Minimum	Maximum
Community college	$363.64	$0.00	$0.00	$4,000.00
4-year BA- or MA-granting college	$1,200.00	$0.00	$0.00	$5,000.00
PhD-granting college or research university	$0.00	$0.00	$0.00	$0.00

Table 80.1.3 How much does the library plan to spend in the next year on tablet computers? Broken out by full-time equivalent enrollment of the college.

Enrollment	Mean	Median	Minimum	Maximum
Less than 2,500	$142.86	$0.00	$0.00	$1,000.00
2,500 to 7,499	$571.43	$0.00	$0.00	$4,000.00
7,500 or more	$1,250.00	$0.00	$0.00	$5,000.00

Table 80.1.4 How much does the library plan to spend in the next year on tablet computers? Broken out by public or private status of the college.

Public or Private	Mean	Median	Minimum	Maximum
Public	$600.00	$0.00	$0.00	$5,000.00
Private	$333.33	$0.00	$0.00	$1,000.00

Table 80.1.5 How much does the library plan to spend in the next year on tablet computers? Broken out by annual full-time tuition prior to any deductions.

Tuition	Mean	Median	Minimum	Maximum
Less than $5,000	$444.44	$0.00	$0.00	$4,000.00
$5,000 to $14,999	$1,000.00	$0.00	$0.00	$5,000.00
$15,000 or more	$250.00	$0.00	$0.00	$1,000.00

Table 81 How much does the library plan to spend in the next year on e-book reading devices?

Table 81.1.1 How much does the library plan to spend in the next year on e-book reading devices?

	Mean	Median	Minimum	Maximum
Entire sample	$0.00	$0.00	$0.00	$0.00

Table 82 Does the library use any outsourced or cloud computing services on which to store metadata, files, special collections, or any other information?

Table 82.1.1 Does the library use any outsourced or cloud computing services on which to store metadata, files, special collections, or any other information?

	No Answer	Yes	No
Entire sample	0.00%	33.33%	66.67%

Table 82.1.2 Does the library use any outsourced or cloud computing services on which to store metadata, files, special collections, or any other information? Broken out by type of college.

Type of College	Yes	No
Community college	18.18%	81.82%
4-year BA- or MA-granting college	33.33%	66.67%
PhD-granting college or research university	57.14%	42.86%

Table 82.1.3 Does the library use any outsourced or cloud computing services on which to store metadata, files, special collections, or any other information? Broken out by full-time equivalent enrollment of the college.

Enrollment	Yes	No
Less than 2,500	25.00%	75.00%
2,500 to 7,499	33.33%	66.67%
7,500 or more	42.86%	57.14%

Table 82.1.4 Does the library use any outsourced or cloud computing services on which to store metadata, files, special collections, or any other information? Broken out by public or private status of the college.

Public or Private	Yes	No
Public	31.58%	68.42%
Private	40.00%	60.00%

Table 82.1.5 Does the library use any outsourced or cloud computing services on which to store metadata, files, special collections, or any other information? Broken out by annual full-time tuition prior to any deductions.

Tuition	Yes	No
Less than $5,000	20.00%	80.00%
$5,000 to $14,999	28.57%	71.43%
$15,000 or more	57.14%	42.86%